THE ESSENTIALS OF THE CLASS OF THE STRONG VERB IN ARABIC

Joyce Åkesson

Pallas Athena

Lund

2010

The Essentials of The Class of The Strong Verb in Arabic

2010 Pallas Athena Distribution, Skarpskyttevägen 10 A, 226 42 Lund, Sweden.

Book design by Joyce Åkesson

ISBN: 978-91-977641-7-9

PRINTED IN THE UNITED STATES OF AMERICA

ALSO BY JOYCE ÅKESSON

Majnūn Leyla: Poems about Passion, Pallas Athena Distribution, December 2009.

The Invitation, Pallas Athena Distribution, July 2009.

Love's Thrilling Dimensions, Pallas Athena Distribution, February 2009.

The Complexity of the Irregular Verbal and Nominal Forms & the Phonological Changes in Arabic, Pallas Athena Distribution, April 2009.

Arabic Morphology and Phonology: Based on the Marāḥ al-Arwāḥ by Aḥmad b. ᶜAlī b. Masᶜūd, Studies in Semitic Languages and Linguistics, Brill Academic Publishers, July 2001.

Aḥmad B. ᶜAlī B. Masᶜūd on Arabic Morphology, Marāḥ al-Arwāḥ: Part 1: The Strong Verb, Studia Orientalia Lundensia, Vol. 4, Brill Academic Publishers, October 1990.

CONTENTS

Preface XI

1. The strong verb, the verbal noun and the derivatives 1

1a. The root 1

1b. The additional segments 2

1c. The question concerning which of the *maṣdar* or verb is the origin of the derivation of the forms 3

a- The Basrans' arguments 3

b- The Kufans' arguments 4

c- The Basrans' answer to the Kufans 5

1d. The *maṣdar* and the derivatives 7

1.1. Form I conjugations of the triliteral verb 8

1.1.1. The derived forms of the triliteral 9

1 - Form II *faᶜᶜala* 10

2 - Form III *fāᶜala* 11

3 - Form IV *ᵓafᶜala* 12

4 - Form V *tafaᶜᶜala* 14

5 - Form VI *tafāᶜala* 15

6 - Form VII *ᵓinfaᶜala* 16

7 - Form VIII *ᵓiftaᶜala* 16

8 - Form IX *ᵓifᶜalla* 17

9 - Form X *ᵓistafᶜala* 17

10 - Form XI *ᵓifᶜālla* 18

11- Form XII *ᵓifᶜawᶜala* 18

1.1.2. The two more anomalous forms 19

1.2. The forms of the quadriliteral 20

1.2.1. Form I of the quadriliteral 21

1.2.1.1. The forms that are coordinated by an augment to Form I *faᶜlala* 21

A- The more uncommon forms 23

a- Forms with prefix before the 1st radical 23

b- Forms with infix after the 1st radical 24

c- Forms with infix after the 2nd radical 24

d- Forms with suffix 25

1.2.2. The derived forms of the quadriliteral 26

1.2.2.1. The forms that are coordinated by more than an augment to Form II *tafaᶜlala* 27

A- Five common patterns are coordinated to it 27

B- The more uncommon forms 28

a- The following form with infix after the 1st radical 28

b- The following forms with infix after the 2nd radical 28

c- The following forms with suffix 29

1.2.2.2. The forms that are coordinated by more than an augment to Form III *ᵓifᶜanlala* 29

1.3. Form I verbal nouns of the triliteral 30

A- The most common forms 30

B- The more uncommon forms 32

1.3.1. Form I verbal nouns formed on the measure of the active participle 33

1.3.1.1. The occurrence of the active participle instead of the *maṣdar* 33

1.3.1.2. The occurrence of the *maṣdar* on the measure of the active participle 35

1.3.2. Form I *verbal nouns* formed on the measure of the passive participle 35

1.3.2.1. The occurrence of the *maṣdar* instead of the passive participle 36

1.3.3. Form I verbal nouns that denote intensity 36

1.3.4. The derived forms of the verbal nouns of the triliteral and Form I and the derived forms of the quadriliteral 37

1.3.4.1. The forms that are analogous with their verbs 38

A- The common forms of the derived forms of the *maṣdar* of the trilateral 38

B- The *maṣdars* of Form I of the quadriliteral and of the derived forms 39

1.3.4.2. The forms that are not analogous with their verbs 40

1.4. The perfect 42

1.4a. *bināᵓ* “undeclinability” and *ᵓiᶜrāb* “declinablility” 42

1.4b. The undeclinability of the perfect 43

1.4.1. The forms of the perfect 46

1.4.1.1. Some remarks concerning the perfect’s forms 46

1.4.1.1.1. The perfect’s 3rd radical is vowelled by a fatḥa 47

1- *faᶜala* 47

2- *faᶜala-t* 47

3- *faᶜal(a)-ā* 48

4- *faᶜala-t(a)-ā* 48

1.4.1.1.2. The perfect’s 3rd radical is vowelled by a ḍamma 49

1- *faᶜal(u)-ū (+ alif mamdūda)* 49

1.4.1.1.3. The perfect’s 3rd radical is vowelless 52

1- *faᶜal-n(a)ā* 53

2- *faᶜal-tum(a)-ā* 53

3- *faᶜal-tum* 55

4- *faᶜal-tunna* 57

5- *faᶜal-na* 58

1.5. The imperfect 59

1.5a. The declinability of the imperfect 59

1.5.1. The forms of the imperfect 62

1.5.1.1. Some remarks concerning its forms 63

1.5.1.1.1. The forms with the imperfect prefixes vowelled by a fatḥa 63

  1- ʾa-fᶜalu 64

  2- ta-fᶜalu 64

  3- ya-fᶜal-na 65

  4- ta-fᶜal(i)-īna, tafᶜal(u)-ūna, yafᶜal(u)-ūna, tafᶜal(a)-āni, yafᶜal(a)-āni 66

  a- The -ī infix in ta-fᶜal(i)-īna and the -ū infix in tafᶜal(u)-ūna and yafᶜal(u)-ūna 66

  b- The -na suffix in ta-fᶜal(i)-īna, tafᶜal(u)-ūna, yafᶜal(u)-ūna, and the -ni suffix in tafᶜal(a)-āni, yafᶜal(a)-āni 67

  c- The -ā infix in the ending -āni in ta-fᶜal(a)-āni and ya-fᶜal(a)-āni 68

  5- na-fᶜalu 69

1.5.1.1.2. The vowelling of the imperfect prefixes with a ḍamma 69

1.5.1.1.3. The vowelling of the imperfect prefixes with a kasra 70

1.6. The imperative 72

1.6a. The undeclinability of the imperative 72

1.6.1. The forms of the imperative 73

1.6.1.1. The *li-* of command 73

1.6.1.2. The vowelling of the prefixed connective hamza of the imperative 74

1.7. The Energetic of the imperfect and imperative 76

1.7.1. The forms of the Energetic 77

1- The Energetic I of the imperfect of the jussive *yafᶜala-nna* 77

2- The Energetic II of the imperfect of the jussive *yafᶜala-n* 78

3- The Energetic I of the imperative *ᵓi-fᶜala-nna* 78

4- The Energetic II of the imperative *ᵓi-fᶜala-n* 79

1.7.1.2. Some remarks concerning some of the Energetic's forms 79

1- The 3rd persons of the masc sing. *ya-f^cala-nna* and *ya-f^cala-n* 80

2- The 3rd persons of the masc pl. *ya-f^calu-nna* and *ya-f^calu-n* 80

3- The 2nd persons of the fem. sing. *ta-f^cali-nna, ta-f^cali-n, ^ɔi-f^cali-nna* and *^ɔi-f^cali-n* 81

4- The 2nd persons of the dual *ta-f^cal(a)-ānni* and *^ɔi-f^cal(a)-ānni* 81

5- The 3rd person of the fem. pl. *ya-f^cal-n(a)-ānni* and *^ɔi-f^cal-n(a)-ānni* 82

1.8. The passive voice 84

1.8.1. The patterns of the derived forms of the triliteral and Form I of the quadriliteral and its derived forms 84

1.8.2. The patterns of Form I of the quadriliteral and its derived forms 85

1.9. The active participle 86

1.9a. The similarity of the active participle to the imperfect 86

1.9.1. The patterns of the groundform 87

1- *fā^cilun* 87

2- *fa^cīlun* 88

3- The forms of intensity 89

1.9.2. The derived forms of the triliteral and the derived forms of the quadriliteral 91

a- The derived forms of the triliteral 92

b- Form I of the quadriliteral and some of its derived forms 93

1.9.2.1. Some anomalous cases 93

1.10. The assimilated adjective 95

1.11. The elative form *ʾafʿalu* 97

1.11.1. Some anomalous cases 97

1.12. The passive participle 100

A- The derived forms of the triliteral 100

B- The groundform and some of the derived forms of the quadriliteral 101

1.13. The nouns of time and place 102

1.14. The noun of instrument 105

PREFACE

This book investigates the class of the strong verb by presenting and analyzing its morphological forms. The verbal forms are the perfect, imperfect, imperative and energetic verbs and the nominal ones are the infinitive noun, active and passive participles and the nouns of time, place and instrument.

It also provides a survey of the theoretical structures by covering different topics that have been taken up in the most representative works of the Classical period from the 8th century until our days, such as the root, the additional segments, the question of the origin of the forms' derivation and the undeclinability of the perfect and imperative and the declinablility of the imperfect and noun.

The linguistic elements and the coverage of the different works offer a rich and complex picture of the Arabic language and make it accessible to both students and researchers of Arabic.

1. The strong verb, the verbal noun and the derivatives

The strong verb, *al-ṣaḥīḥ,* can be defined as the verb which has strong consonants as its three radicals, e.g. *ḍaraba* (cf. for a study Muᵓaddib, *Taṣrīf* 147-184, Ibn Yaᶜīš, *Mulūkī* 38-45, de Sacy, 149-225, Wright, 52-68, Blachère, 38 sqq., Bakkūš, *Taṣrīf* 84-97, ᶜAbd al-Raḥīm, *Ṣarf* 18-21, Åkesson, *Ibn Masᶜūd* fol. 2a-17 b, par. (11)-(168)).

1a. The root:

The form of the verb *ḍaraba* is conformable to *faᶜala.* The root or the lexical meaning of most of the words in Arabic refers to three radicals, which can be represented as *f-ᶜ-l.* The *f* stands for the 1st radical, the *ᶜ* for the 2nd and the *l* for the 3rd radical.

The forms that are generated from the root can have for instance a vowelless radical, e.g. the form *faᶜlun* characteristic for the *maṣdar* "verbal noun", e.g. *qatlun* "killing and of the assimilated adjective, e.g. *šaksun* "perverse, stubborn" or have an additional segment or more inserted in their structures. The additional segments can be prefixes, infixes or suffixes. For instance the additional segment *m* is the prefix of the form of the passive participle *mafᶜūlun* of the noun of time and place *mafᶜalun* and of the noun of instrument *mifᶜalun*. The additional segment *ā* is the infix of the form of the active participle *fāᶜilun* and the additional segment *-ū* is the suffix of the 3rd person of the masc. pl. of the perfect *faᶜal(u)-ū* etc.

1b. The additional segments:

The additional segments are included in the phrase *hawītu l-simāna* "I loved the plump women" with the *waṣla* written before the *l* in *l-sīmāna* counted as a hamza, i.e. *ʾal-sīmāna* -, namely the *h,* the *w,* the *y,* the *t,* the *ʾ*, the *l,* the *s,* the *m,* the *ā* and the *n.* This phrase ocurs in this verse said by al-Māzinī and cited by Ibn Ǧinnī, *de Flexione* 9, *Munṣif I,* 98, Ibn Yaᶜīš, IX, 141, *Mulūkī* 100, Ibn Masᶜūd, fol. 11b-12a, Howell, IV, fasc. I, 1096:

"Hawītu l-simāna fa-šayyabnanī
wa-qad kuntu qidman hawītu l-simāna"
"I loved the plump women, and they turned me hoary,
and I had of old loved the plump women".

1c. The question concerning which of the maṣdar or verb is the origin of the derivation of the forms:

The basic verbal structure that is chosen for the verb is *faᶜala.* The *maṣdar* of Form I has many measures, e.g. *fiᶜlun, faᶜlun* etc.

The question concerning which of the *maṣdar* or verb should be considered as the origin of the derivation of all the forms has been debated in detail by the Basrans and Kufans (cf. e.g. Zağğāğī, *Īḍāḥ* 56-63, Zamaḫšarī, 16-18, Ibn al-Anbārī, *Inṣāf* Q. 28, 102-107, ᶜUkbarī, *Masāʾil* 68-76, Ibn Yaᶜīš, I, 110 sqq., de Sacy, I, 278-280, Lane, II, 1662).

a- The Basrans' arguments:

The Basrans include the verb among the derivatives and choose the *maṣdar* as the origin of the derivation.

Their main argument is their concept of the *maṣdar's* oneness contra the verb's plurality. By this they mean that the *maṣdar* does not distinguish between the tenses like the verb does because it points to an unlimited time, has only one pattern, e.g. *al-ḍarbu* "the hitting" and *al-qatlu* "the killing" and points only to the happening.

As for the verb it is divided into three tenses: *māḍī* "perfect", *ḥāḍir* "present" (for discussions concerning it see Zağğāğī, *Īḍāḥ* 86-88, Ibn Yaᶜīš, VII, 4) and *mustaqbal* "imperfect". It points to a fixed time, has many patterns and points to two things: the happening and the time. According to Ibn al-Anbārī, *Inṣāf* Q. 28, 103, the *maṣdar's* reference to an unlimited time characterizes it as *al-muṭlaq* "the absolute" whereas the verb's reference to a limited time characterizes it as *al-muqayyad* "the limited". The Basrans' logical conclusion is that just as the absolute is the origin of the limited and the number one is the origin of the number two, the *maṣdar* is the origin of derivation of the verb.

b- The Kufans' arguments:

The Kufans include the *maṣdar* among the derivatives and choose the verb as the origin of the derivation. As one of their arguments, they stress the idea of the dependence of the *maṣdar* on the verb regarding the unsoundness or the soundness of the weak consonant in its structure. If a phonological change due to the unsoundness of the weak segment is carried out in the verb, then a phonological change is carried out as well in the *maṣdar.* An example of a verb with the 1st radical *w* unsound is *ya*^{c}*idu* "he promises" in the imperfect, underlyingly *yaw*^{c}*idu,* in which the *w* is elided, which determines that its *maṣdar* is ^{c}*idatun* "a promise" underlyingly *wi*^{c}*dun* in which the *w* is elided as well. If the weak consonant remains sound in the verb it remains as well sound in the *maṣdar.* Some examples of verbs in which the weak segment is sound are *yawǧalu* (cf. Sībawaihi, II, 266, Zamaḫšarī, 178) and *qāwama,* both which retain their 2nd radical *w.* It is this soundness of the weak segment in the verb that leads consequently according to the Kufans, to its soundness in the *maṣdar's* structure, i.e. *waǧalun* and *qiwāmun* respectively.

c- The Basrans' answer to the Kufans:

According to the Basrans, the phonological change of the unsound weak consonant that is carried out in the *maṣdar,* which is on the analogy of the one that is carried out in the verb, is only due to avoid a certain heaviness in its structure (for their arguments see Ibn al-Anbārī, *Inṣāf* 105) and does not point to the origin or derivative. In order to defend their theory, they take up the example *ya*^{c}*idu* "he promises" underlyingly *yaw*^{c}*idu,* in which the *w* is elided because it occurs between the *y* and the kasra, which causes a heaviness in the structure. The *w* is also elided from *ta^cidu* "/2 masc. sing." and "/3 fem. sing." underlyingly *taw^cidu,* in spite of the fact that it does not occur between the *y* and the kasra, so that it is similar in its form to *ya^cidu.* Another example is *ʾukrimu* underlyingly *ʾuʾakrimu* "I honour", in which one of both hamzas is elided because of the heaviness of both their combination. It is also elided from *tukrimu* "/2 masc. sing." and "/3 fem. sing." underlyingly *tuʾakrimu,* in spite of the fact that two hamzas are not combined in them, by analogy to *ʾuʾakrimu.* This does not mean that the 3rd person *ya^cidu* or the 1st person *ʾuʾakrimu* is the base form of the remaining persons.

Furthermore another Basran argument that can be added here against the Kufan one, is that there exists verbs in which the weak consonant is unsound whereas the weak consonant of their *maṣdars* is sound. An example is *wa^cada* "to promise" that loses its 1st radical *w* in the imperfect *ya^cidu,* but that has also the *maṣdar wa^cdun* with the 1st radical *w* retained, and *wazana* "to balance" that loses its 1st radical *w* in the imperfect *yazinu,* but that has the maṣdar *waznun* “a balance” with the 1st radical *w* retained (cf. Zaǧǧāǧī, *Īḍāḥ* 60, ^cUkbarī, *Masāʾil* 75). This means that the soundness or unsoundness of a weak consonant in the verb is not a necessary condition for the soundness or the unsoundness of a weak consonant in the *maṣdar.*

1d. The maṣdar and the derivatives:

The Basrans who consider the *maṣdar* as the origin of the derivation, present nine derivatives of the *maṣdar,* including among them the tenses of the verbs and the class of the prohibition that is particular to them. The derivatives are generally the measures of the perfect, namely *faᶜala,* or the measures of the maṣdar, namely *fiᶜlun, faᶜlun* etc., the imperfect, namely *yafᶜalu,* the imperative, namely *ᵓifᶜal,* the prohibition, namely *lā tafᶜal,* the active participle, namely *fāᶜilun,* the passive participle, namely *mafᶜūlun,* the noun of time, namely *mafᶜalun,* the noun of place, namely *mafᶜalun* and the noun of instrument, namely *mifᶜalun.*

1.1. Form I conjugations of the triliteral verb

The well-known conjugations of the triliteral can conveniently be divided into six ones:

1- *faᶜala yafᶜilu*, e.g. *ḍaraba yaḍribu* "to hit".

2- *faᶜala yafᶜulu*, e.g. *qatala yaqtulu* "to kill". There exist some anomalous cases as *faḍila yafḍulu* "to remain", which should have occurred formed according to this conjugation, namely *faḍala yafḍulu*, but which instead has *faḍila* in the perfect with the kasra given to the 2nd radical. Concerning it Sībawaihi, II, 240 remarks that it is an anomaly, and that preferably *faḍala yafḍulu* is more fit to be used according to the analogy. Other examples are *ḥadira yaḥḍuru* "to be present" and *naᶜima yanᶜamu* and *yanᶜumu* "to be affluent".

3- *faᶜila yafᶜalu*, e.g. *ᶜalima yaᶜlamu* "to know".

These first three conjugations are termed as *daᶜāʾim al-ʾabwāb* "the pillars of the conjugations" by Ibn Masᶜūd (cf. Åkesson, *Ibn Masᶜūd* 50: fol. 3b) because of the variation of the vowels of their 2nd radical in the perfect and in the imperfect and because of their numerousness.

4- *faᶜala yafᶜalu*, e.g. *fataḥa yaftaḥu* "to open". As a general rule, we can observe that when the 2nd or 3rd radical of the verb is a guttural consonant, namely *a* ᵓ, *h*, ᶜ, *ḥ*, *ġ* or *ḫ*, the 2nd radical of the imperfect is vowelled by a fatḥa (cf. Sībawaihi, II, 270-272). Some anomalies occur however in which the imperfect's vowel can be a fatḥa or a kasra, e.g. *naᶜaqa yanᶜaqu* or *yanᶜiqu* "to croak", or a fatḥa or a ḍamma, e.g. *salaḫa yaslaḫu* or *yasluḫu* "to flay" (cf. Wright, II, 58). An anomalous verb which pertains to this conjugation is *rakana yarkanu* "to lean", which does not have any guttural consonant as a 2nd or 3rd radical. It could be a combination of two forms (cf. ibid) or of two dialectal varieties (cf. Lane, I, 1148).

5- *faᶜula yafᶜulu,* e.g. *karuma yakrumu* "to be generous". This conjugation denotes the quality and is intransitive.

6- *faᶜila yafᶜilu,* e.g. *ḥasiba yaḥsibu* "to assume". Vollers, *Volkssprache* 129 notes that Ibn ᶜAmir, Ḥamza and ᶜĀṣim read *yaḥsabu* instead of *yaḥsibu* from all the surs. of the Qurᵓān.

1.1.1. The derived forms of the triliteral

The common derived forms of the triliteral (for a study see Zamaḫšarī, 126-130, Vernier, I, 125-150, Howell, II-III, 245-279, Wright, II, 29-47, Blachère, 38-73, Roman, *Étude* II, 917-947, Fleisch, *Traité II,* 227-340, Åkesson, *Ibn Masᶜūd* 113 sqq. (39, b)) are the following:

1 - Form II *fa*$^{c\,c}$*ala.*

An example is *qaṭṭa*^{c}*a* "to cut". Its meaning:

1- It intensifies the meaning of the root.

2- It can be similar to the groundform, e.g. *zaltuhu* and *zayyaltuhu* "I separated it" (cf. Zamaḫšarī, 129, Howell, II-III, 271). It can also have its meaning or the meaning of Form V, e.g. *badala, baddala* and *tabaddala* "to exchange". Some verbs are also intransitive (cf. Blachère, 51).

3- It makes causative transitive verbs, e.g. ^{c}*alima* "to know" in the groundform, ^{c}*allama* "to teach".

4- It indicates the time when a thing is done, e.g. *ṣabbaḥnā massaynā wa-saḥḥarnā* "we went to find him in the morning, in the evening and at dawn" (cf. Sībawaihi, II, 251).

5- It has an estimative meaning, e.g. *ṣadaqa* "to believe" in the groundform, *ṣaddaqa* "to consider as sincere", and *kaḏiba* "to lie" in the groundform, *kaḏḏaba* "to consider as a liar".

6- It makes someone or something do a thing, e.g. *kattaba* "to make someone write".

7- It is derived from nouns and expresses their meanings, e.g. *ḫubzun* "bread", *ḫabbaza* "to bake bread" (cf. Vernier, I,138).

8- It expresses the negation of the idea existing in the groundform, e.g. *fazi*^{c}*a* "to fear", *fazza*^{c}*a* "to deliver from fear" (cf. ibid, I,138).

9- It expresses a blessing, e.g. *saqqaytuhu wa-ra*^{cc}*aytuhu* " I said to him: *saqyan wa-ra*^{c}*yan* "May God preserve you and give you rain" (cf. Sībawaihi, II, 249, Howell, II-III, 271, Vernier, I, 138).

10- It denotes a movement from one place to another, e.g. *šarraqa* "to go to the Orient", *ġarraba* "to go to the Occident" (cf. Vernier, I,137) and *kawwafa* "to go to al-Kūfa" (cf. Howell, II-III, 271).

11- It denotes becoming its root, e.g. ^{c}*ağğazati l-marʾatu* "the woman became a ^{c}*ağūzun* "an old woman" (cf. ibid, II-III, 271).

2 - Form III *fā*^{c}*ala.*

An example is *qātala* "to fight". Its meaning:

1- It denotes the idea of reciprocity, e.g. *ḍārabtuhu* "I hit him and he hit me" (cf. Sībawaihi, II, 253).

2- It denotes the idea of rivality, e.g. *šarufa* "to be high-ranking" in the groundform, *šārafa* "to vie for precedence in honor or nobility" (cf. Vernier, I, 139).

3- It denotes enduring the action of the groundform, e.g. *qasā (*with final *alif mamdūda)* "to be harsh" and *qāsā* (with final *alif maqṣūra)* "to suffer" (cf. ibid, I, 139).

4- It comprehends the meaning of the prepositions, e.g. *ǧalasa ^{c}inda l-sulṭāni and ǧālasa l-sulṭāna* "he sat near the sultan" (cf. ibid, I, 138-139).

5- It can be similar to the groundform, e.g. *safara* and *sāfara* "to go forth to journey" (cf. Zamaḫšarī, 129, Howell, II-III, 272).

6- It can be similar to Form II *fa^{cc}ala,* e.g. *ḍā^{c}aftu* "I doubled [the thing]", like *ḍa^{cc}aftuhu* (cf. Zamaḫšarī, 129, Howell, II-III, 273).

7- It can be similar to Form IV *ʾaf^{c}ala,* e.g. *rā^{c}inā sam^{c}aka* "make your ear to be possessed of mindfulness for us", like *ʾar^{c}inā* (cf. Howell, II-III, 272).

3 - Form IV *ʾaf^{c}ala.*

An example is *ʾakrama* "to honour". Its meaning:

1- It can be formed from nouns, e.g. *ʾaqfara* "to become a desert" from *qafrun* "desert", *ʾarāba* "to incur suspicion" from *raybun* "suspicion" (cf. Sībawaihi, II, 250, Howell, II-III, 272, Vernier, I, 140).

2- It denotes entering a place or time, e.g. *ʾanǧada* "to enter Naǧd", *ʾaǧbala* "to enter the mountain" and *ʾaṣbaḥa* "to enter upon the morning" (cf. Howell, II-III, 267, Vernier, I, 140).

3- It denotes moving from one place to another, e.g. *ʾaḥǧaza* "he went to al-Ḥiǧāz" and *ʾaġraba* "he went to the Occident" (cf. Vernier, I, 140-141).

4- It denotes finding a quality in the object, e.g. *ʾaḥmadtuhu* "I found him such as to be praised" (cf. Zamaḫšarī, 128, Howell, II-III, 268).

5- It denotes exposing (for discussions see Larcher, *ʾAfʿala* 7 sqq.), e.g. *ʾaqtaltuhu* "I exposed him to slaughter" and *ʾabaʿtuhu* "I exposed him to sale" (cf. Zamaḫšarī, 128, Howell, II-III, 267).

6- It denotes depriving, e.g. *ʾaškaytuhu* "I removed his complaint" (cf. Zamaḫšarī, 129, Howell, II-III, 268).

7- It denotes negating the groundform, e.g. *šaqā* (with final *alif maqṣūra)* "to be cured" and *ʾašqā* (with final *alif maqṣūra)* "not to be cured" (cf. Vernier, I, 140).

4 - Form V *tafa^{cc}ala.*

An example is *tafaḍḍala* "to deign". Its meaning:

1- It is the reflexive to Form II *fa^{cc}ala,* e.g. *kassartuhu fa-takassara* "I broke it in pieces and it broke in pieces" (cf. Zamaḫšarī, 127, Howell, II-III, 261).

2- It denotes affecting, e.g. *tašağğa^{c}a* "he encouraged himself", or endeavouring to acquire, e.g. *taḥallama* "he endeavoured to acquire forbearance" (cf. Sībawaihi, II, 255, Zamaḫšarī, 127, Howell, II-III, 261-262).

3- It is similar to Form X *$^{\circ}$istaf^{c}ala,* with its two meanings of believing and requiring, e.g. *takabbara* "he believed himself to be great" and *tabayyanahu* "he sought the settlement and manifestation of it" (cf. Zamaḫšarī, 127-128, Howell, II-III, 262).

4- It denotes a repeated action that occurs progressively in time, e.g. *tağarra^{c}ahu* "he swallowed it in successive gulps" (cf. Zamaḫšarī, 127, Howell, II-III, 263).

5- It denotes taking for oneself, e.g. *tadayyartu l-makāna* "I took the place for an abode" and *tawassadtu l-turāba* "I took the dust for a pillow" (cf. Zamaḫšarī, 128, Howell, II-III, 263).

6- It denotes associating with a religion, a sect, a nation or a tribe, e.g. *tanaṣṣara* "to become a Christian", *tahawwada* "to become a Jew", *taqayyasa* "to associate with the Qaisī tribe", *taᶜarraba* "to become an Arab" and *tašaᵓᵓama* "to become a Syrian" (cf. Vernier, I, 143).

7- It denotes abstaining from the action of the groundform, e.g. *tahağğada* "to stay awake at night" and *taḥawwaba* "to abstain from sin" (cf. Zamaḫšarī, 128, Vernier, I, 143).

5 - Form VI *tafāᶜala.*

An example is *taḍāraba* "to strike". Its meaning:

1- It denotes an action done by two and more, e.g. *taḍārabā* "they both fought together" and *taḍārabū* "they fought together" (cf. Zamaḫšarī, 128, Howell, II-III, 265).

2- It is similar to the groundform, e.g. *tawānaytu* "I flagged in the matter" (cf. Zamaḫšarī, 128, Howell, II-III, 264).

3- It is the reflexive of Form II *faᶜᶜala,* e.g. *ᶜaẓẓamtuhu fa-taᶜaẓẓama* "I glorified him and he was glorified" (cf. Vernier, I, 143).

4- It is the reflexive of Form III *fā^cala,* e.g. *bā^cadtuhu fa-tabā^cada* "I made him to remove to a distance, and he removed to it" (cf. Zamaḫšarī, 128, Howell, II-III, 265).

5- It is similar to Form VIII *ʾifta^cala,* e.g. *taḍārabū* and *ʾiḍṭarabū* "they hit each other", and *taqātalū* and *ʾiqtatalū* "they killed each other" (cf. Sībawaihi, II, 254).

6- It denotes stimulating an action or a state, e.g. *taǧāhaltu* "I feigned to be ignorant" (cf. Zamaḫšarī, 128, Howell, II-III, 264).

6 - Form VII *ʾinfa^cala.*

An example is *ʾinṣarafa* "to depart". Its meaning:

1- It is the passive of the groundform *fa^cala,* e.g. *kasartuhu fa-nkasara* "I broke it and it broke" (cf. Sībawaihi, II, 252, Zamaḫšarī, 129, Howell, II-III, 273).

7 - Form VIII *ʾifta^cala.*

An example is *ʾiḥtaqara* "to despise". Its meaning:

1- It is similar to the groundform, e.g. *kasaba* and *ʾiktasaba* "to obtain" (cf. Zamaḫšarī, 129, Howell, II-III, 276, Vernier, I, 145).

2- It is the reflexive of the groundform, e.g. *samiᶜa* "to hear" and *ᵓistamaᶜa* "to listen to" and *ǧamaᶜa* "to collect" and *ᵓiǧtamaᶜa* "to collect themselves".

3- It is similar to Form VI *tafāᶜala*, e.g. *taqātalū* "they killed each other" and *ᵓiqtatalū* and *taǧāwarū* and *ᵓiǧtawarū* "they became mutual neighbours" (cf. Sībawaihi, II, 254).

4- It is similar to Form VII *ᵓinfaᶜala,* e.g. *ġamamtuhu fa-ġtamma wa-nġamma* "I grieved him and he grieved" (cf. Sībawaihi, II, 252, Zamaḫšarī, 129, Howell, II-III, 274).

5- It denotes making for oneself, e.g. *ᵓištawā* "to roast meat" (cf. Sībawaihi, II, 256, Zamaḫšarī, 129, Howell, II-III, 275).

8 - Form IX *ᵓifᶜalla.*

An example is *ᵓiḥmarra* "to be red". Its meaning:

1- It is used for permanent colours or defects.

9 - Form X *ᵓistafᶜala.*

An example is *ᵓistaḫraǧa* "to remove". Its meaning:

1- It is similar to the groundform, e.g. *qarra* and *ᵓistaqarra* "to rest" (cf. Zamaḫšarī, 130, Howell, II-III, 277).

2- It denotes the request of the act, e.g. *ᵓistaᶜmalahu* "he required his working" (cf. Sībawaihi, II, 255, Zamaḫšarī, 130, Howell, II-III, 277).

3- It denotes becoming transmuted, e.g. *ᵓistaḥǧara l-ṭīnu* "the clay became stone" (cf. Zamaḫšarī, 130, Howell, II-III, 277).

4- It denotes finding someone to be of a certain quality, e.g. *ᵓistaᶜẓamtuhu* "I found him to be grand" (cf. Zamaḫšarī, 130, Howell, II-III, 278).

5- It denotes appointing someone for a position, e.g. *ᵓistawzara* "to appoint one as a minister" (cf. Vernier, I, 146).

10 - Form XI *ᵓifᶜālla.*

An example is *ᵓiḥmārra* "to be very red". Its meaning:

1- It intensifies Form IX *ᵓifᶜalla.*

11- Form XII *ᵓifᶜawᶜala:*

An example is *ᵓiᶜšawšaba* "to cover with luxuriant herbage". Its meaning:

1- It denotes intensity.

12- Form XIII *ʾifʿawwala,* e.g. *ʾiǧlawwaḏa* "to last long".

1.1.2. The two more anomalous forms

13- Form XIV: *ʾifʿanlala,* e.g. *ʾisḥankaka* "to be dark".

14- Form XV *ʾifʿanlā,* e.g. *ʾiḥbanṭā* "to be swollen or filled with rage".

1.2. The forms of the quadriliteral

The strong verb's quadriliteral (for a general study see Zamaḫšarī, 130, Vernier, I, 150-154, Howell, II-III, 280-282, Wright, II, 47-49, Blachère, 73-76, Roman, *Étude II,* 982-983, Fleisch, *Traité II,* 427-463, Åkesson, *Ibn Mas^{c}ūd* 123 sqq. (41)) can generally be:

1- a combination of well-known syllables in common expressions, e.g. *basmala* "to say *bi-smi l-lāhi* 'in the name of God'".

2- a repeated biliteral root expressing a sound or a movement, e.g. *zalzala* "to shake".

3- a triliteral verb that has been developed through the insertion of one augment resulting in a form that is identical in its structure to Form I *fa^{c}lala*, .e.g. *zaḥlafa* "to roll along" from *zaḥafa* "to advance slowly", or the insertion of two augments resulting in forms that are coordinated to Form II *tafa^{c}lala,* e.g. *tağalbaba* "to put on a *ğilbābun* 'garment'" from *ğalaba* "to bring", or more than two augments resulting in forms that are coordinated to Form III *$^\supset$if^{c}anlala.*

The development of the triliteral verb into being of four, five, or six segments, is named according to de Sacy, I, 125 *al-mulḥaqāt bi-l-rubā^{c}ī* "commensurable to be coordinated with the quadriliteral" (for a study of these forms see. Ibn ᶜUṣfūr, I, 167 sqq., Suyūṭī, *Muzhir II,* 27-28).

4- formed from foreign words of more than three segments, e.g. *tasarwala* "to put on *sarāwīlu* 'trousers or drawers'" from the Persian *šalwār.*

1.2.1. Form I of the quadriliteral

One common Form I of the quadriliteral exists, namely:

1- Form I *faᶜlala,* e.g. *daḥraǧa* "to roll".

1.2.1.1. The forms that are coordinated by an augment to Form I faᶜlala:

There exist six common patterns that are coordinated by an augment to Form I *faᶜlala,* but the list can be made much longer.

1- *faᶜlala* with the two last radicals identical, e.g. *šamlala* "to gather ripe dates and also to be active or nimble".

2- *fawᶜala* with the infixed *w* after the 1st radical, e.g. *ḥawqala* meaning *lā ḥawla wa-lā quwwata ʾilla bi-l-lāhi* "there is no power and no strength save in God". It is a combination of syllables in a frequently used expression. Other examples similar to *ḥawqala* in being a combination of syllables in well-known expressions, but which are formed according to *fa^{c}lala* and not to *faw^{c}ala,* are *basmala* "to say *bi-smi l-lāhi* "in the name of God", *ǧa^{c}fada* "to say *ǧu^{c}iltu fidāka* "may I become your ransom!", *ḥasbala* "to say *ḥasbī l-lāhu* "God is sufficient for me" and *ḥamdala* "to say *al-ḥamdu li-l-lāhi* "praise belongs to God".

3- *fay^{c}ala* with the infixed *y* after the 1st radical, e.g. *bayṭara* "to practise the veterinary art or farriery" and *^{c}aṯyara* "to stumble".

4- *fa^{c}wala* with the infixed *w* after the 2nd radical, e.g. *ǧahwara* "to utter one's speech in a loud voice".

5- *fa^{c}nala* with the infixed *n* after the 2nd radical, e.g. *qalnasa* "to put on a cap called *qalansuwa".*

6- *fa^{c}lā* with the suffixed *alif maqṣūra* after the 3rd radical, e.g. *qalsā* "to put on a cap called *qalansuwa".*

A- The more uncommon forms:

a- Forms with prefix before the 1st radical:

7- the *t: taf^{c}ala,* e.g. *tarmasa* "to absent oneself from battle" from *ramasa* "to conceal" (cf. Volck/Kellgren, *Ibn Mālik* 10, Suyūṭī, *Muzhir II,* 27, Howell, II-III, 255).

8- the *s: saf^{c}ala,* e.g. *sanbasa* "to hasten" from *nabasa* (cf. Suyūṭī, *Muzhir II,* 27, Volck/Kellgren, *Ibn Mālik* 9, Howell, II-III, 255, Wright, II, 47).

9- the *^{c}: ^{c}af^{c}ala,* e.g. *zahzaqa* "to laugh much" i.e. *$^{\supset}$ahzaqa* (cf. al-Ḫalīl in his introduction to the *Kitāb al-^{c}ayn* translated by Haywood, *Lexicography* 32, Volck/Kellgren, *Ibn Mālik* 9, Ibn Manẓūr, III, 1878, Howell, II-III, 254, Wright, II, 48).

10- the *h: haf^{c}ala,* e.g. *halqama* "to swallow" (cf. Suyūṭī, *Muzhir II,* 27, Howell, II-III, 255).

11- the *m: maf^{c}ala,* e.g. *marḥaba* "to welcome" (cf. Suyūṭī, *Muzhir II,* 27).

12- the *n: naf^{c}ala,* e.g. *narǧasa* "to be dirty" (cf. ibid, 27).

13- the *y: yaf^{c}ala,* e.g. *yarna$^{\supset}$a* "to dye red with henna" (cf. ibid 27).

<u>b- Forms with infix after the 1st radical:</u>

14- The ^{c}: *fa^{c}lala,* e.g. *ṯa^{c}ǧara* "to shed blood or something else" (cf. Fleisch, *Traité II,* 441; for more examples concerning this particular form see 441-442).

15- the *m: fam^{c}ala* (cf. Suyūṭī, *Muzhir II,* 27), e.g. *zamlaqa* "to eject (the stallion) its semen before insertion" (cf. Volck/Kellgren, *Ibn Mālik* 10, Howell, II-III, 255).

16- the *n: fan^{c}ala* (cf. Volck/Kellgren, *Ibn Mālik* 10, Suyūṭī, *Muzhir II,* 27), e.g. *danqa^{c}a l-rağulu* "the man became poor and clave to the earth" (cf. Ibn ^{c}Uṣfūr, I, 171, Howell, II-III, 257).

17- the *h: fah^{c}ala* (cf. Suyūṭī, *Muzhir II,* 27), e.g. *rahmasa* "to conceal" from *ramasa* (cf. Volck/Kellgren, *Ibn Mālik* 9, Howell, II-III, 255; for more examples concerning this particular form see Fleisch, *Traité II,* 440-441).

<u>c- Forms with infix after the 2nd radical:</u>

18- the $^{\supset}$: *fa$^{c\supset}$ala,* e.g. *bar$^{\supset}$ala l-dīku* "the cock ruffled the feathers of his neck" (cf. Howell, II-III, 257).

19- the *t: fa^{c}tala,* e.g. *kaltaba* "to act with slyness" (cf. Volck/Kellgren, *Ibn Mālik* 10, Howell, II-III, 255).

20- the ^{c}*: fa^{cc}ala,* e.g. *ḫay^{c}ala* "to walk slowly because of a disturbance" (cf. Fleisch, *Traité II,* 442. For more examples concerning this particular form see 442-443).

21- the 1st radical: *fa^{c}fala,* e.g. *zahzaqa* in the meaning of *ʾazhaqa* "to destroy" (cf. Suyūṭī, *Muzhir II,* 27). However, according to Ibn Manẓūr, III, 1878 and others already mentioned, *zahzaqa* is in the meaning of *ʾahzaqa* "to laugh boisterously, which classifies it under ^{c}af^{c}ala mentioned above.

22- the *m: fa^{c}mala,* e.g. *ǧalmaṭa* "to shave (one's head)" from *ǧalaṭa* (cf. Howell, II-III, 255, Wright, II, 47).

23- the *y: fa^{c}yala* (cf. Suyūṭī, *Muzhir II,* 27), e.g. *^{c}aḏyaṭa* "(a man) stooled in coition" (cf. Volck/Kellgren, *Ibn Mālik* 9, Howell, II-III, 255).

d- Forms with suffix:

24- the *r: fa^{c}lara,* e.g. *šamḫara* "to be proud" from *šamaḫa* "to be high" (cf. Fleisch, *Traité II,* 444).

25- the *s: fa^{c}lasa,* e.g. *ḫalbasa* "to seduce and take away" from *ḫalaba* "to delude" (cf. Volck/Kellgren, *Ibn Mālik* 9, Suyūṭī, *Muzhir II,* 27, Howell, II-III, 254, Wright, II, 47, Fleisch, *Traité II,* 444).

26- the *l: fa^{c}lala,* e.g. *šam^{c}ala* "to spread itself" from *šama^{c}a* "to be scattered" (cf. Wright, II, 47, Fleisch, *Traité II,* 443).

27- the *m: fa^{c}lama,* e.g. ġalṣama "cut his epiglottis" from ġalaṣa (cf. Volck/Kellgren, *Ibn Mālik* 10, Suyūṭī, *Muzhir II,* 27, Howell, II-III, 255; for more examples concerning this particular form see Fleisch, *Traité II,* 443-444).

28- the *n: fa^{c}lana,* e.g. *qaṭrana* "to smear (the camel) with pitch" from *qaṭara* (cf. Suyūṭī, *Muzhir II,* 27, Volck/Kellgren, *Ibn Mālik* 9, Howell, II-III, 255, Wright, II, 48).

1.2.2. The derived forms of the quadriliteral

Three derived forms are common. A 4th more anomalous form exists as well. They are the following:

1- Form II *tafa^{c}lala,* e.g. *tadaḥraǧa* "to roll along".

2- Form III *ʾifᶜanlala,* e.g. *ʾiḥranǧama* "to gather together in a mass".

3- Form IV *ʾifᶜalalla,* e.g *ʾiqšaᶜarra* "to shudder with horror".

4- Form V *ʾifᶜallala,* e.g. *ʾihrammaᶜa* "to be fast in the race".

<u>*1.2.2.1. The forms that are coordinated by more than an augment to Form II tafaᶜlala:*</u>

<u>A- Five common patterns are coordinated to it</u>

1- *tafaᶜlala* with the prefixed *t* and the two last radicals identical, e.g. *taǧalbaba* "to put on a *ǧilbābun*".

2- *tafawᶜala* with the prefixed *t* and the infixed *w* after the 1st radical, e.g. *taǧawraba* "to put on a *ǧawrābun,* "a sock" from the root *ǧ r b.*

3- *tafayᶜala* with the prefixed *t* and the infixed *y* after the 1st radical, e.g. *tašayṭana* "to act like a devil" from the root *š ṭ n.*

4- *tafa^{c}wala* with the prefixed *t* and the infixed *w* after the 2nd radical, e.g. *tarahwaka* "to show a feebleness in one's walk" from the root *r h k.*

5- *tamaf^{c}ala* with the prefixed *t* and the infixed *m* before the 1st radical, e.g. *tamaskana* "to become poor" from the root *s k n.*

B- The more uncommon forms:

a- The following form with infix after the 1st radical:

6- the *h: tafah^{c}ala,* e.g. *tarahšafa* "to suck" from *rašafa* (cf. Volck/Kellgren, *Ibn Mālik* 9, Howell, II-III, 255).

b- The following forms with infix after the 2nd radical:

7- the *n: tafa^{c}nala,* e.g. *taqalnasa* "to put on oneself a cap" (cf. Ibn ^{c}Uṣfūr, I, 168, Suyūṭī, *Muzhir II,* 27).

8- the *y: tafa^{c}yala,* e.g. *tarahya^{c}a* "(the clouds) moved, and were prepared for the rain" (cf. Ibn Manẓūr, III, 1748).

c- The following forms with suffix:

9- the *t: tafa*^{c}*lata,* e.g. *ta*^{c}*afrata* "to act as a devil" (cf. Suyūṭī, *Muzhir II,* 27, Wright, II, 48).

10- the *l: tafa*^{c}*lala,* e.g. *tašama*^{c}*ala* "to disperse itself" from *šama*^{c}*a* (for discussions see Fleisch, *Traité II,* 443).

11- the *alif maqṣūra: tafa*^{c}*lā* (cf. Suyūṭī, *Muzhir II*, 27), e.g. *tasalqā* "to be thrown down upon one's back" from *salqā* (cf. Volck/Kellgren, *Ibn Mālik* 10, Howell, II-III, 255).

1.2.2.2. The forms that are coordinated by more than an augment to Form III ^{ɔ}*if*^{c}*anlala:*

Two common patterns are coordinated to it:

1- ^{ɔ}*if*^{c}*anlasa* with the prefixation of the hamza, the infixation of the *n* after the 2nd radical and the suffixation of the *s,* e.g. ^{ɔ}*iq*^{c}*ansasa* "to have a hump in front" from the root *q* ^{c} *s.*

2- ^{ɔ}*if*^{c}*anlā* with the prefixation of the hamza, the infixation of the *n* after the 2nd radical and the suffixation of the *alif maqṣūra,* e.g. ^{ɔ}*islanqā* "to lay on one's back" from the root *s l q.*

1.3. Form I verbal nouns of the triliteral

The *maṣdar* "verbal noun" is termed by Sībawaihi, I, 11 as *ᵓism al-ḥadaṯ* "the noun of the action", or *ᵓism al-ḥadaṯ wa-l-ḥadaṯāna* "the noun of both the action and the accident (of the agent)" (cf. Zamaḫšarī, 16).

Zamaḫšarī, 96-97 cites thirty-two forms among which some pertain to other forms than the strong verb, Wright, I, 111-112 mentions fourty-four, Howell, I, fasc. IV 1516-1517 mentions fourty-six forms and Ibn Mālik, *Lāmīya* verse 62-70 mentions fourty-nine forms.

<u>A- The most common forms:</u>

1- *faᶜlun* e.g. *qatlun* "killing".

2- *fiᶜlun* e.g. *fisqun* "profligacy".

3- *fuᶜlun* e.g. *šuġlun* "occupying".

4- *faᶜlatun* e.g. *raḥmatun* "having mercy".

5- *fiᶜlatun* e.g. *nišdatun* "seeking".

6- *fuᶜlatun* e.g. *kudratun* "being turbid".

7- *faᶜlā* e.g. *daᶜwā* "praying".

8- *fiᶜlā* e.g. *ḏikrā* "remembering".

9- *fuᶜlā* e.g. *bušrā* "announcing happy news".

10- *faᶜlānun* e.g. *layyānun* "softening".

11- *fiᶜlānu* e.g. *ḥirmānu* "refusing".

12- *fuᶜlānu* e.g. *ġufrānu* "forgiving".

13- *faᶜalānu* e.g. *nazawānu* "escaping".

14- *faᶜalun* e.g. *ṭalabun* "demanding".

15- faᶜilun e.g. *ḫaniqun* "strangling".

16- *fiᶜalun* e.g. *ṣiġarun* "being small".

17- *fuᶜlan* e.g. *hudan* "guiding".

18- *faᶜalatun* e.g. *ġalabatun* "overcoming".

19- *faᶜilatun* e.g. *sariqatun* "stealing".

20- *faᶜālun* e.g. *ḏahābun* "going away".

21- *fiᶜālun* e.g. *ṣirāfun* "being in heat".

22- *fuᶜālun* e.g. *suʾālun* "requesting".

23- *fa^cālatun* e.g. *zahādatun* "abstinence".

24- *fi^cālatun* e.g. *dirāyatun* "knowing".

25- *fu^cūlun* e.g. *duḫūlun* "entering".

26- *fa^cūlun* e.g. *qabūlun* "accepting".

27- *fa^cīlun* e.g. *wağīfun* "beating of the heart".

28- *fu^cūlatun* e.g. *ṣuhūbatun* "being reddish".

29- *maf^calun* e.g. *madḫalun* "entering".

30- *maf^cilun* e.g. *marği^cun* "retreating".

31- *maf^cālun* e.g. *mas^cātun* "endeavouring".

32- *maf^cilatun* e.g. *maḥmidatun* "praising".

<u>B- The more uncommon forms:</u>

33- *fa^calūtun* e.g *ğabarūtun* "being haughty".

34- *fu^calniyatun* e.g. *bulanhiyatun* "ease".

35- *taf^calatun, taf^cilatun* or *taf^culatun* e.g. *tahlakatun, tahlikatun* or *tahlukatun* "perishing".

36- *fuᶜullatun* e.g. *ġulubbatun* "overcoming".

37- *fuᶜullā* (with final *alif maqṣūra)* e.g. *ġulubbā* (with final *alif maqṣūra)*.

38- *fuᶜlalun* e.g. *sūdadun* "being lord".

39- *tufᶜalun* e.g. *tudraᵓun* "ability to repel foes".

40- *fayᶜalūlatun* e.g. *kaynanūnatun* "being".

41- *faᶜlūlatun* e.g. *ṣayrūratun* "becoming".

42- *faᶜīlatun* e.g. *šabībatun* "becoming adolescent.

43- *fāᶜūlatun* e.g. *ḍārūratun* "affliction".

44- *mafāᶜilatun* e.g. *masāᵓiyatun* "displeasing".

1.3.1. Form I verbal nouns formed on the measure of the active participle

Form I *maṣdar* can be formed on the measure of the active participle *fāᶜilun.* An example of such a *maṣdar* is *qāᵓiman* which is used instead of *qiyāman* in the phrase *qumtu qāᵓiman* "I rose a rising" (cf. Wright, II, 132), in which it is a *maṣdar* formed according to the measure of the active participle *fāᶜilun.* It occurs as well in the example *qum qāᵓiman* that is said instead of *qum qiyāman* in this verse cited by Ibn Fāris, *Ṣāḥibī* 237 who discusses the active participle as a substitute for the *maṣdar:*

> *"Qum qāʾiman qum qāʾiman*
> *laqīta ʿabdan nāʾiman*
> "Get up! Get up!
> You met a sleeping slave!".

1.3.1.1. The occurrence of the active participle instead of the maṣdar:

The active participle occurs also instead of the *maṣdar* in the following verse said by Bišr b.Abī Ḫāzim praising Aus b. Ḥāriṯa b. Laʾm al-Ṭāʾī, cited by Zamaḫšarī, 97, Ibn Yaʿīš, VI, 51, Howell, I, fasc. IV, 1557, in which *kāfī* occurs anomalously in the nominative instead of the *kāfiyan,* the *y* being made vowelless by poetic licence, in the meaning of *kifāyatan:*

> *"Kafā bi-l-naʾyi min ʾasmāʾa kāfī*
> *wa-laysa li-ḥubbihā ʾiḏ ṭāla šāfī"*.
> "Sufficient indeed [for me as a trial] is the distance from Asmāʾ;
> and there is no healer for the love of her, since it has lasted long".

1.3.1.2. The occurrence of the maṣdar on the measure of the active participle:

The *maṣdar* can occur on the measure of the active participle *fāʿilatun* (for a study see Ibn Fāris, *Ṣāḥibī* 237, Zamaḫšarī, 97, Ibn Yaʿīš, VI, 50-52) as in the sur. 69: 8 *(fa-hal tarā lahum min bāqiyatin)* "Then seest thou any of them left surviving?", in which *bāqiyatin* has the meaning of *baqāʾin,* in the sur. 56: 2 *(laysa li-waqʿatihā kāḏibatun)* "Then will no (soul) entertain falsehood", in which *kāḏibatun* has the meaning of *kaḏibun* and in the sur. 69: 4 *(fa-ʾammā ṯamūdu fa-ʾuhlikū bi-l-ṭāġiyati)* "But the Thamūd, - they were destroyed by a terrible storm of thunder and lightning!", in which *bi-l-ṭāġiyati* has the meaning of *bi-l-ṭuġyāni.*

1.3.2. Form I verbal nouns formed on the measure of the passive participle

Form I *maṣdar* can be formed on the measure of the passive participle *mafʿūlun.* An example of such a maṣdar is *al-maftūnu* that occurs instead of *al-fitnatu* in the sur. 68: 6 *(bi-ʾayyikumu l-maftūnu)* "Which of you is afflicted with madness" (cf. Ibn Fāris, *Ṣāḥibī* 237, Zamaḫšarī, 98 , Ibn Yaʿīš, VII, 53, Åkesson, *Ibn Masʿūd* 50: fol. 3b), in which it is a *maṣdar* formed according to the measure of the passive participle *mafʿūlun.*

1.3.2.1. *The occurrence of the maṣdar instead of the passive participle:*

The pattern of the *maṣdar* can occur instead of the pattern of the passive participle, and has its meaning (for some cases of the active and passive partiple occurring instead of the *maṣdar* and vice versa see Wright, II, 132-133), as in the sur. 31: 11 *(haḏā ḫalqu l-lāhi)* "Such is the Creation of God", in which *ḫalqu* occurs instead of *maḫlūqu* "the created".

1.3.3. Form I verbal nouns that denote intensity

Some Form I *maṣdars* denote multiplication and intensification (for them see Sībawaihi, II, 261, Zamaḫšarī, 98, Ibn Yaʿīš, VI, 55-56, Volck/Kellgren: *Ibn Mālik* 22, Åkesson, *Ibn Masʿūd 50:* fol. 3b, ibid, 105-106: (25), Wright, II, 116-117). The common ones are the following:

1- *tafʿālun,* e.g. *tahdārun* "much fermentation" and *talʿābun* "intensive sporting". The pattern *tifʿālun* with the *t* given the kasra does not denote intensification, and the two examples that are known to be formed according to it are *tibyānun* "explanation" which occurs in the sur. 16: 89 *(wa-nazzalnā ʿalayka l-kitāba tibyānan li-kulli šayʾin)* "And We have sent down to thee the Book explaining all things" and *tilqāʾun* "meeting" which occurs in the meaning of *laqyānun* "meeting" in a verse said by al-Rā'ī, cited by Howell, I, fasc. IV, 1561: *Fa-l-yawma qaṣṣara ᶜan tilqā'ika l-'amalu* "For today hope has fallen short of meeting you".

2- *fiᶜᶜīlā* [with final *alif maqṣūra],* e.g. *al-ḥiṯṯīṯā* "much incitement (cf. Ibn Manẓūr, II, 773, Lane, I, 512) " and *al-dillīlā* "much guidance " (cf. Ibn Manẓūr, II, 1414, Lane, I, 901). Other examples are *qittītā* "much mischief-making", *hiǧǧīrā* "much evil-speaking" and *ḫillīfā* "being much engrossed with the business of the *Ḫilāfa"* (cf. Daqr, *Muᶜǧam 57).* The last example occurs in the saying said by ᶜUmar in the tradition *lawlā l-ḫillīfā la-'aḏḏantu* "Had I not been much engrossed with the buisness of the Ḫilāfa, I would chant the call to prayer".

1.3.4. The derived forms of the verbal nouns of the triliteral and Form I and the derived forms of the quadriliteral

The forms of the maṣdar of the derived forms of the triliteral and of Form I and the derived forms of the quadriliteral verb are divided between those that are analogous and those that are not analogous with their verbs.

1.3.4.1. The forms that are analogous with their verbs

Many of the forms of the *maṣdar* of the derived forms of the triliteral and of Form I and the derived forms of the quadriliteral verb (for a study see Ibn Mālik, *Lāmīya* 246-249, Volck/Kellgren, *Ibn Mālik* 20-23, Howell, I, fasc. IV, 1529-1545, Wright, II, 115-118) are analogous with their verbs. The reason of this resemblance in forms is according to Ibn Yaᶜīš, VI, 47, that these verbs' forms follow special measures and do not vary as the forms of Form I of the triliteral of which the vowel of the 2nd radical in many cases alternate in the perfect and in the imperfect.

Some of the forms of the *maṣdar* of the derived forms of the triliteral and of the quadriliteral that follow the specific forms of verbs, are presented in the following manner by Zamaḫšarī, 97:

> *"ᵓafᶜala ᵓifᶜālun, ᵓiftaᶜala ᵓiftiᶜālun, ᵓinfaᶜala ᵓinfiᶜālun, ᵓistafᶜala ᵓistifᶜālun, ᵓifᶜalla ᵓifᶜilālun, ᵓifᶜālla ᵓifᶜīlālun, ᵓifᶜawwala ᵓifᶜiwwālun, ᵓifᶜawᶜala ᵓifᶜīᶜālun, ᵓifᶜanlala ᶜifᶜinlālun, tafāᶜala tafāᶜulun* and *ᵓifᶜalalla ᵓifᶜillālun".*

A- The common forms of the derived forms of the *maṣdar* of the triliteral:

1- Form II: *tafᶜīlun, tafᶜilatun, tafᶜulatun, tafᶜālun, tifᶜālun fiᶜᶜālun, fiᶜᶜilayun* and *fiᶜᶜīlāᵓu.*

2- Form III: *mufāᶜalatun, fiᶜālun, fīᶜālun* and *fiᶜᶜālun.*

3- Form IV: *ᵓifᶜālun.*

4- Form V: *tafaᶜᶜulun* and *tifiᶜᶜālun.*

5- Form VI: *tafāᶜulun, tafāᶜalun* and *tafāᶜilun.*

6- Form VII: *ᵓinfiᶜālun.*

7- Form VIII: *ᵓiftiᶜālun* and *fiᶜᶜālun.*

8- Form IX: *ᵓifᶜilālun.*

9- Form X: *ᵓistifᶜālun.*

10- Form XI: *ᵓifᶜīlālun.*

11- Form XII: *ᵓifᶜīᶜālun.*

12- Form XIII: *ᵓifᶜiwwālun.*

13- Form XIV: *ᵓifᶜinlālun.*

14- Form XV: *ᵓifᶜinlāᵓun.*

B- The *maṣdars* of Form I of the quadriliteral and of the derived forms:

1- Form I: *faᶜlalatun, fiᶜlālun* and *faᶜlālun.*

2- Form II: *tafa*^{c}*lulun.*

3- Form III: ^{ɔ}*if*^{c}*inlālun.*

4- Form IV: ^{ɔ}*if*^{c}*illālun.*

1.3.4.2. The forms that are not analogous with their verbs

Some of the common forms (for a study see Zamaḫšarī, 97, Ibn Ya^{c}īš, VI, 47-50) are the following:

1- *fi*^{cc}*ālun,* e.g. *killāmun* "a talk", from Form II *kallama* "to talk to". The pattern occurs by the Yemenites (cf. Rabin, 37). Another example is *kiḏḏābun* which occurs in the sur. 78: 28 *(wa-kaḏḏabū bi-*^{ɔ}*āyātinā kiḏḏāban)* "But they (impudently) treated our signs as false".

2- *fi*^{c}*ālun* and *fī*^{c}*ālun,* e.g. *qitālun* and *qītālun* "a fight, a battle" from Form III *qātala* "to fight against".

3- *tifi*^{cc}*ālun,* e.g. *tiḥimmālun* "a burden" from Form V *taḥammala* "to burden oneself". Another example that can be added is *timillāqun* "affection", which occurs in this verse said by an unknown poet, cited by Zamaḫšarī, 97, Ibn Ya^{c}īš, VI, 47, IX, 157, *Mulūkī* 194, Howell, I, fasc. IV, 1538, Åkesson, *Ibn Mas*^{c}*ūd* 107-108):

"Ṯalāṯatu ᵓaḥbābin fa-ḥubbun ᶜalāqatun
wa-ḥubbun timillāqun wa-ḥubbun huwa l-qatlu".
"There are three loves; for there is a love that is
attachment,
and a love that is affection, and a love that is murder".

4 - *fiᶜlālun,* e.g. *zilzālun* "a concussion, convulsion, an earthquake" from Form I of the quadriliteral *zalzala* "to shake".

1.4. The perfect

The perfect verb, *al-māḍī*, is the verb that refers to an action that occurred in the past. It is *mabnī* "undeclinable" and takes suffixes which refer to the tense, number, gender and person.

1.4a. Binā᾽ "undeclinability" and ᾽iᶜrāb "declinablility":

In the field of syntax, *binā᾽* "uninflectedness, undeclinability, invariability" (for definitions see de Sacy, I, 395, Lane, I, 260) implies that the word's ending is invariable whereas *iᶜrāb* "inflection, declension" suggests that the ending's state varies in accordance with the operator governing it (for discussions concerning both these terms see Bohas/Kouloughli, *Linguistic* 53-55).

Iᶜrāb can as well refer to the formal *iᶜrāb,* which is the complete vowelling of the word (cf. ᶜUkbarī, *Masā᾽il* 102-105, Owens, *Foundations* 40). Thus the formal *᾽iᶜrāb* is different from the syntactical *᾽iᶜrāb,* as the latter is mainly concerned with the ending of the declinable word in accordance with its operator's rule (cf. Carter, *Linguistics [Širbīnī, Āǧurrūmīya]* 37: 2. 15 (1)).

The question concerning which of the three parts of speech, the noun, verb or particle, is entitled to be declinable or undeclinable, has been a debated subject by many Arab grammarians (e.g. Zağğāğī, *Īḍāḥ* 77-82; for discussions see Versteegh, *Zağğāğī* 127-128). The declension has been given principally to the nouns whereas the undeclinability has been given to the verbs, - with the exception of the imperfect -, and to the particle.

1.4b. The undeclinability of the perfect:

The reason why the perfect is undeclinable and why its marker of undeclinability is a vowel, namely the fatḥa, is that the perfect is partly similar to the noun. Its vowelling separates it from the undeclinable imperative, which does not present any similarity with the noun, and which for this reason is given a marker that does not exist in the noun, namely the sukūn (for discussions see Ibn Yaᶜīš, VII, 4-5).

The following arguments are introduced concerning the reasons of its undeclinability:

1- Like the noun it can function as a modifier, *ṣifah,* to the indefinite noun. This is remarked in the sentence *maratu bi-rağulin ḍaraba wa-ḍāribin* "I passed by a man who hit and who was hitting", in which both the perfect *ḍaraba* and the active participle of the noun *ḍāribin* have the same function (cf. ibid 4).

2- In the same manner as the active participle, it can function as a *ḫabar* "predicate" in a nominal sentence. An example is *zaydun qāma* "Zaid was getting up", in which the perfect *qāma* is a predicate to the topic Zaydun in the same manner as the active participle *qā*ᵓ*imun* is a predicate to the same topic in the sentence *Zaydun qā*ᵓ*imun.*

3- It can as well have the same meaning as the imperfect, which is considered to be the form that is similar to the declinable noun, and thus can replace it. For instance in a sentence as ᵓ*in qumta qumtu* "If you rise, I shall rise", the perfects *qumta qumtu* that occur after the conditional ᵓ*in* can be used instead of the imperfect forms *taqum* ᵓ*aqum* after the same conditional, i.e. ᵓ*in taqum* ᵓ*aqum.*

4- A resemblance that exists between the perfect and the active participle form of the noun, is that the active participle refers to past time when it is used as the first element of an ᵓ*iḍāfa* construction, as in e.g. ᵓ*anā qātilu ġulāmika* "I am the killer of your servant", in which the active participle *qātilu* that is put in the nominative before the noun in the genitive *ġulāmika,* shows that the action of the killing is completed, in the same manner as *qataltu* does in the sentence ᵓ*anā qataltu ġulāmaka* "I have killed your servant". The difference between the perfect and the active participle is that the active participle that occurs as a first element of an *ʾiḍāfa* construction, and thus refers to a completed action in the past, is unable to govern the noun after it in the accusative as the perfect does, so *ʾanā qātilu ġulāmika* is said for this meaning and not *ʾanā qātilu ġulāmaka* (cf. Suyūṭī, *Ašbāh III,* 535-536).

According to the theory of Ibn Yaᶜīš, VII, 5, the reason why the perfect's ending is given a fatḥa and not a ḍamma, is that some Arabs used the ḍamma instead of the *ū* to mark the pl., e.g. *qāmu* said instead of *qāmū* "they rose /masc. pl.". Another example is *kānu* said instead of *kānū* in the following verse said by an anonymous poet, cited by Muʾaddib, *Taṣrīf* 15, Ibn Yaᶜīš, VII, 5, Ibn Ḫālawaihi, *Qirāʾāt* I, 352, Ibn al-Anbārī, *Inṣāf* Q. 72, 222 and Howell, I, fasc. II, 517 with *wa-law* instead of *fa-law:*

> *"Fa-law ʾanna l-ʾaṭibbāʾī kānū ḥawlī*
> *wa-kāna maᶜa l-ʾaṭibbāʾI l-ʾusātu"*
> "O, if the physicians had been around me
> and the surgeons were with the physicians!"

Other examples with the ḍamma replacing the suffixed pronoun of the nominative, the *ū,* presented by Muʾaddib, *Taṣrīf* 296 are *lam yaḏhabu ʾiḫwatuka* "your brothers did not go" said by some Arabs with *lam yaḏhabu* instead of *lam yaḏhabū.*

Some read as well the sur. 53: 31 as *(li-yağziya l-laḏīna ʾasāʾu)* "So that He rewards those who do Evil" with *ʾasāʾu* instead of *ʾasāʾū.*

1.4.1. The forms of the perfect

The forms of the perfect *faʿala* are the following:

	sing.	dual	pl.
1st	*faʿal-tu*		*faʿal-n(a)ā*
2nd masc.	*faʿal-ta*	*faʿal-tum(a)-ā*	*faʿal-tum*
2nd fem.	*faʿal-ti*	*faʿal-tum(a)-ā*	*faʿal-tunna*
3rd masc.	*faʿala*	*faʿal(a)-ā*	*faʿal(u)-ū (+ ā)*
3rd fem.	*faʿala-t*	*faʿal(a)-t(a)ā*	*faʿal-na*

1.4.1.1. Some remarks concerning the perfect's forms:

The forms that are taken up at first are those in which the perfect's 3rd radical is vowelled. This vowel can be a fatḥa or a ḍamma. The forms of which the 3rd radical is vowelless are then presented.

1.4.1.1.1. The perfect's 3rd radical is vowelled by a fatḥa:

The fatḥa vowels the 3rd radical in the 3rd person of the masc. sing. *faᶜala*, the 3rd person of the fem. sing. *faᶜala-t* and the 3rd person of the masc. dual *faᶜal(a)-ā* and fem. dual *faᶜal(a)-t(a)ā.*

1- *faᶜala:*

As stated previously, the perfect's marker of undeclinability is a fatḥa.

2- *faᶜala-t:*

The vowelless suffix *-t* in the 3rd person of the fem. sing. *faᶜala-t* marks the fem. and is not a pronoun. It can be compared to the vowelled suffix *-t* of the 1st and 2nd persons of the sing., namely the *-tu* in *faᶜal-tu* "I did", the *-ta* in *faᶜal-ta* "/2 masc. sing." and the *-ti* in *faᶜal-ti* "/2 fem. sing.".

The proof of it being a marker of the feminine is that if it had been a pronoun it would have been elided by the manifested agent that can follow it (cf. Åkesson, *Ibn Masᶜūd* 64: fol. 9a) as it is impossible to combine two agents for the same verb. As an example *ḍaraba-t Hindun* "Hind hit" can be mentioned, in which the *-t* marker of the fem. in *ḍaraba-t* is not elided by the agent following it, i.e. *Hindun*, as *ḍaraba Hindun* is not accepted. No agent pronoun is suffixed to this form of the fem. as the *-t* suffix is a marker of the fem., and alike the 3rd person of the masc. sing. *faᶜala,* the agent is considered as latent (cf. Versteegh, *Language* 81).

We can remark that the elision of the agent pronoun is by contrast carried out when the perfect's form of the 3rd person of the masc. pl. is combined with a separated agent following it, as it looses its *-ū* agent suffix to hinder the combination of two agents, e.g. *ḍaraba l-awlādu* is said instead of *ḍarabū l-ʾawlādu* "the children hit".

3- *faᶜal(a)-ā:*

There exists a similarity between the suffix *-ā* of the dual of the 3rd person of the masc. *faᶜal(a)-ā* and the suffix *-ā* of the dual of the 3rd person of the masc. of the independent pronoun of the nominative of the 3rd person of the masc. sing. *hum(a)-ā* "they both /dual".

4- *faᶜala-t(a)-ā:*

The infix *-t* marker of the fem. sing. in the 3rd person of the dual of the fem. pl. *faᶜala-t(a)ā* is underlyingly vowelless alike the suffix *-t* in the 3rd person of the fem. sing. *faᶜala-t.* It is however given a fatḥa to hinder the combination of two vowelless segments, as it precedes the vowelless *ā*. Hence *faᶜala-t(a)-ā* is said and not *faᶜala-t-ā.*

It can be noted that the suffix *-ā* of the dual of the 3rd person of the fem. sing. in *faᶜala-t(a)ā* is the same as the one in the 3rd person of the masc. sing. *faᶜal(a)-ā.*

1.4.1.1.2. The perfect's 3rd radical is vowelled by a ḍamma:

The ḍamma vowels the 3rd radical in the 3rd person of the masc. pl. *faᶜal(u)-ū.*

1- *faᶜal(u)-ū (+ alif mamdūda):*

The ḍamma vowels generally the 3rd radical in the 3rd person of the masc. pl. *faᶜal(u)-ū (+ alif mamdūda)* "they did /masc. pl.". Concerning the suffix *-ū (+ alif mamdūda)* in *faᶜal(u)-ū (+ alif mamdūda),* we observe that it is the same as the *-ū* suffix of the base form of the pronoun of the nominative of the 3rd person of the masc. pl. *hum(u)-ū (+ alif mamdūda)* "they /masc. pl.".

The rule of having a ḍamma preceding the *-ū* suffix *(+ alif mamdūda)* is not followed when it concerns a verb with 3rd weak radical of the conjugation *fa^c^ala* of which the 3rd weak radical is elided, e.g. *rama-w (+ alif mamdūda)* "they threw /masc. pl.".

The *alif mamdūda* suffixed after the *ū* of the pl. is termed as *alif al-wiqāya* "the guarding alif" (cf. Wright, I, 11). There exist different opinions concerning its occurrence.

According to al-Farrā°'s theory, this alif is suffixed after the -*ū* of the pl., so that it is possible to differentiate between the *ū* which is a radical in verbs with 3rd weak radical and the *ū* marking the pl. As an example of a verb in the sing. ending with a *w* radical, *yad^c^ū* "he calls" can be mentioned, and as an example of a verb in the jussive ending with the suffixed pronoun of the nominative of the masc. pl., the *ū,* preceding the *alif mamdūda, lam yad^c^ū* "they did not call" can be mentioned. Had it not been for the *alif madmdūda,* then both the singular and the pl. would be mixed together.

Some Arabs use defectively the indicative mood of the sing. in some cases of weak 3rd radical verbs instead of the correct jussive mood (for a study of such cases see Zamaḫšarī, 184-185, Ibn Ya^c^īš, X, 104-107, Wright, IV 389) by maintaining the 3rd weak radical instead of eliding it. An example is *lam yad^c^ū* "he did not call" with the maintainance of the *ū* said instead of the correct *lam yad^c^u* (cf. Åkesson, *Ibn Mas^c^ūd,* fol. 5a) with its elision. Had it not been for the *alif mamdūda* after the *ū*, then both the sing., i.e. *lam yad*ᶜ*ū* "he did not call" in this defective dialectal variant, and the pl., i.e. *lam yad*ᶜ*ū* (with the *alif mamdūda* after the *ū)* "they did not call" would have been mixed up together.

This defective maintainance of the *ū* in the jussive occurs in this verse said by an unknown poet, cited by Zamaḫšarī, 184, Ibn Yaᶜīš, X, 104, Howell, IV, fasc. I, 1576 and Wright, IV 389, in which *lam tahǧū* occurs instead of *lam tahǧu:*

> *"Haǧawta Zabbāna ṯumma ǧiʾta muᶜtaḏiran*
> *min haǧwi Zabbāna lam tahǧū wa-lam tadaᶜi".*
> "You did satirize Zabbān: then you came, apologizing
> for satirizing Zabbān: you did not satirize [him], nor did
> you leave [him] alone".

According to the theory of al-Aḫfaš, the alif is suffixed so that the wāw of the pl. is not mixed up with the wāw of the conjunction (cf. ᶜAbd al-Tawwāb's note on Rāzī, in Ḫalīl b. Aḥmad ..., *Ḥurūf* 135). An example is the phrase *ḥḍrwtkllm* (cf. Åkesson, *Ibn Mas*ᶜ*ūd* 54: fol. 5a) written without diatritic signs and without an alif after the *w*. It can be read in two manners: *ḥaḍara wa-takallama* "He came and talked" or *ḥaḍarū takallama* "they came, he talked" causing an inevitable confusion, which is why the presence or the absence of the alif after the *w* is significant.

1.4.1.1.3. The perfect's 3rd radical is vowelless:

The 3rd radical of the perfect's basic form *fa^{c}al-* is given a sukūn when the vowelled agent suffixes, the *-t:* i.e. *tu, ta* and *ti,* and the *-n:* i.e. *na,* are attached to it.

These forms are: *fa^{c}al-tu* "I did", *fa^{c}al-ta* "/2 masc. sing.", fa^{c}al-ti "/2 fem. sing.", *fa^{c}al-tum(a)ā, fa^{c}al-tum, fa^{c}al-tunna, fa^{c}al-n(a)ā* "/1 pl." and *fa^{c}al-na* "/3rd fem. pl.".

The reason of the vowellness of the 3rd radical is to hinder the forbidden combination of four consecutive vowels (for this principle see Zaǧǧāǧī, *Īḍāḥ* 75, Ḥassān, *Uṣūl* 228). Hence *fa^{c}al-tu, fa^{c}al-ta, fa^{c}al-ti, fa^{c}al-nā and fa^{c}al-na* are said and not *fa^{c}ala-tu, fa^{c}ala-ta, fa^{c}ala-ti, fa^{c}ala-nā* and *fa^{c}ala-na.*

The perfect's 3rd radical is not vowelless when the pronoun of the accusative is suffixed to it, e.g. *ḍaraba-ka* "he hit you /masc. sing." which is said with the succession of the four vowels, and not *ḍarab-ka.* The reason why the Arab grammarians accept the succession of the four vowels in *ḍaraba-ka* is that they consider the suffixed pronoun of the agent as one with its verb, whereas they consider the suffixed pronoun of the object as another word separated from it, thus leading to a proper rule as the acceptance of the succession of the four vowels. The verb is in need of an agent, manifest or suppressed, which is why the verb is considered as one with its pronoun of the agent, whereas it can manage without an object, which is the reason why it and its pronoun of the object are considered as two separate words (cf. Ibn Ǧinnī, *Sirr I,* 221).

1- *faᶜal-n(a)ā:*

There exists a similarity between the *-n* infix in the perfect's form of the 1st person of the pl. *faᶜal-n(a)ā* "we did" and the first consonant *n* of the independent pronoun of the agent of the 1st person of the pl. *naḥnu* "we" (cf. Åkesson, *Ibn Masᶜūd* 58: fol. 6b). The *-ā* ending in it is formed according to the ending in the independent pronoun of the 1st person of the pl. *ᵓinnanā* "we" and is, on the other hand, necessary to differenciate it from the *-na* that marks the 3rd person of the fem. pl. in the perfect form *faᶜal-na* "they did /fem. pl.".

2- *faᶜal-tum(a)-ā:*

The perfect's forms of the duals of the 2nd person of the masc. and of the fem. sing. *faᶜal-tum(a)-ā* "you did /masc. or fem. dual" are common.

The *-m* infix is added to the perfect's form before the dual *-ā* suffix so that there is no confusion between the pronoun's ending *-tum(a)ā* of the 2nd person of the dual and the pronoun's ending *-t(a)ā* of the 2nd person of the masc. sing. to which the alif of saturation can in some cases, as in poetry and in pause, be suffixed to (cf. Åkesson, *Ibn Masᶜūd* 56-58: fol. 5b). In other words the *-m* infix is added to avoid confusing the alif of the dual with the alif of saturation (cf. Ibn al-Anbārī, *Inṣāf* Q. 96, 284).

An example that can be taken up with the alif of saturation suffixed to the pronoun of 2nd person of the masc. sing. is *ᵓant(a)ā* said instead of *ᵓanta,* which occurs in the following verse cited by ibid, Q. 96, 284, Åkesson, *Ibn Masᶜūd* 56: fol. 5b):

> *"ᵓAḫūka ᵓaḫū mukāšaratin wa-ḍiḥkin*
> *wa-ḥayyāka l-ᵓālihu fa-kayfa ᵓantā?".*
> "Your brother is one who cleaves to cheerfulness and laughter
> And may God preserve your life, in which condition are you in?".

Another example occurs in this verse said by Sālim b. Dāra, cited by Muᵓaddib, *Taṣrīf* 25, Ibn al-Anbārī, *Inṣāf* Q. 45, 144, Q. 96, 284 and Åkesson, *Ibn Masᶜūd* 148: (60):

"Yā Murra yā bna Wāqi^cin yā ʾantā
ʾanta l-laḏī ṭallaqta ʿāma ǧuʿtā".
"O Murr, O Ibn Wāqiʿ, O you!
It is you who divorced [your wife] in a year when you were hungry!".

The pronoun's ending *-tum(a)-ā* in the perfect's form *faʿal-tum(a)-ā* is the same as the ending of the independent pronoun of the masc. and fem. of the dual *ʾantum(a)-ā* (cf. Åkesson, *Ibn Masʿūd* 56: fol. 5b). There exists as well a similarity between the dual ending *-m(a)-ā* in *ʾantum(a)-ā* "you both" and the ending *-m(a)ā* of the independent pronoun of the 3rd person of the dual *hum(a)ā* "they both" (cf. ibid, 56-58: fol. 5b-6a).

3- *faʿal-tum:*

The *-tum* ending in the perfect's of the 2nd person of the masc. pl. *faʿal-tum* is formed according to the ending *-tum(a)ā* in the perfect's form of the 2nd person of the masc. pl. *faʿal-tum(a)ā*. The *-tum* ending is underlyingly *-tum(u)ū* (+ *alif mamdūda*), and hence *faʿal-tum* is underlyingly *faʿal-tum(u)ū* (+ *alif mamdūda*).

The *-ū* suffix following the infix *-tum* is elided because of the dislike that the Arabs have for pronouns or nouns ending with an *-ū* preceded by a ḍamma, which they deem as a heavy combination. We can remark that the *-ū* suffix of the perfect's form of the 3rd person of the masc. pl. *fa^{c}al(u)ū* is not elided as it is not attached to a pronoun infix, but follows immediately the 3rd radical (cf. ibid, 58: fol. 6a).

Hence the only pronoun which exists in the language with a *w* preceded by a ḍamma is *huwa* "he" (cf. ibid). In the light of this principle that nouns cannot end with a *w* preceded by a ḍamma in nouns, the formation of the pl. of the noun *dalwun* "bucket" is *ʾadlin* and not *ʾadluwun* (cf. Ibn Ǧinnī, *de Flexione* 43, Zamaḫšarī, 185, Ibn Ya^{c}īš, X, 107-108, Ibn Mālik, *Alfīya* 147, Goguyer's commentary to verse 617, Lane, I, 909, Wright, II, 209).

The verbs however can end with a *w* preceded by a ḍamma (cf. Ibn Ǧinnī, *de Flexione* 42-43, Ibn Ya^{c}īš, X, 104) without that this combination is deemed as heavy, e.g. the imperfect's form of the 3rd person of the sing. *yaġz(u)ū* "he assaults" underlyingly *yaġz(u)w* and *yad^c(u)ū* "he calls" underlyingly *yad^c(u)w* before that the assimilation of the *w* to the *u* is carried out resulting in the lengthened *ū*.

The *-ū* suffix of the base form *fa^{c}al-tum(u)ū,* which is elided resulting in *fa^{c}al-tum*, is however maintained when a pronoun of the accusative is attached to the verb, because the *-ū* is not longer at the extremity of the word. An example is *ḍarab-tumū-hu* "you hit him /masc. pl." with the *-hu* object pronoun suffixed to it. Furthermore the pronoun of the accusative is also a reason why the verb is brought back to its base form (cf. Ibn Yaᶜīš, III, 95), as by principle the pronouns bring back the words to their base form (cf. Sībawaihi, I, 341-342).

4- *faᶜal-tunna:*

The *-na* suffix in the ending *-tunna* of the perfect's form of the 2nd person of the fem. pl. *faᶜal-tunna* is doubled differently from the *-na* suffix in the perfect's form of the 3rd person of the fem. pl. *faᶜal-na.*

According to a theory presented by Ibn Masᶜūd (cf. Åkesson, *Ibn Masᶜūd* 58: fol. 6b), its base form is *ḍarab-tum-na* with the *-na* marker of the fem. pl. following the suffixed pronoun of the 2nd person of the masc. pl. *-tum.* Then the *m* was assimilated to the *n* because of the proximity of the *m* to the *n* in the point of utterance, as the *m* originates between the lips and the *n* from the upper part of the nose. This interchange of the *m* for the *n* and vice versa is remarked for instance in *ᶜanbarun* that becomes *ᶜambarun.*

According to another theory, the reason why the *n* is doubled in the ending *-tunna* of the 2nd person of the fem. pl. is that two nūns should arise as compared in number to the *m* and the *ū* in the ending *-tum(u)ū* of the 2nd person of the masc. pl. *faᶜal-tum(u)ū* (cf. Ibn Yaᶜīš, III, 87, Howell, I, fasc. II, 516).

5- *faᶜal-na:*

There exists a similarity between the suffix *-na* in the the 3rd person of the fem. pl. of the perfect *faᶜal-na* and the suffix *-na* of the independent pronoun of the nominative (cf. Åkesson, *Ibn Masᶜūd* 54: fol. 5a) of the 3rd person of the fem. pl. *hun-na* "they /fem. pl.".

1.5. The imperfect

The imperfect verb, *al-muḍāri*[c] refers to an action that can be incomplete, is still going on, or is carried out in the present, past or future time. It is declinable for mode and takes prefixes and in some cases as well infixes and suffixes which refer to the agent.

1.5a. The declinability of the imperfect:

The imperfect is declinable and vowelled by a ḍamma as its marker of declinability due to its resemblance to the active participle which pertains to the noun category and which is declinable (cf. Ibn Ya[c]īš, VII, 6, Åkesson, *Ibn Mas*[c]*ūd* 66: fol. 9b, Owens, *Foundations* 207-208).

So generally stated, the reason why the imperfect is declinable is its resemblance to the active participle form of the noun, which is a noun.

These are the principal arguments:

1- The phonological form of the imperfect *yaḍribu* and the active participle *ḍ(a)āribun* are commensurable regarding the vowelling or the vowellessness of both these forms' respective consonants (cf. Owens, *Foundations* 208).

2- Just like the active participle, the imperfect can occur as a modifier, *ṣifat,* of an indefinite noun. In a sentence as *hāḏā rağulun yaḍribu* "this is a hitting man", the imperfect that follows the indefinite noun functions as a modifier, and corresponds in its meaning to the modifier in the example *hāḏā rağulun ḍāribun* (cf. ibid).

3- The inceptive *la-* which is specific to be prefixed to nouns which it emphasizes, e.g. *ʾinna Zaydan la-qāʾimun* "verily Zaid is getting up", can be prefixed to the imperfect, i.e. *ʾinna Zaydan la-yaqūmu,* and the meaning is the same. This particular *la* cannot be made to precede the perfect, i.e. *ʾinna Zaydan la-qāma* with the very same specific meaning that this affirmative la- introduces.

4- The imperfect can be general, by which it is meant that it is vague, because it can be valid for the tenses of the present and future (cf. Ibn Ḫālawaihi, *Iʿrāb* 4), e.g. *yaḍribu* can mean "he hits, he is hitting or he shall hit". It is this vagueness that is considered as similar to the vagueness of the indefinite noun, e.g. *raʾaytu rağulan* "I saw a man", in which *rağulan* "a man" refers to an indefinite man.

5- The prefixation of the *s* or *sawfa* to the imperfect specifies its meaning by making it refer to a special tense which is the future, e.g. *Zaydun sa-yaḍribu* and *sawfa yaḍribu* "Zaid will hit", in the same manner as the prefixation of the definite article *l-* to the indefinite noun renders it definite, e.g. *raᵓaytu l-rağula* "I saw the man".

6- The imperfect functions as a *ḥāl* "denotative of state", in e.g. *Zaydun yaḍribu,* and corresponds in its function and meaning to the active participle, in e.g. *Zaydun ḍāribun* "Zaid is hitting".

7- The dual and pl. suffixes. respectively *-āni* and *-ūna* of the imperfect and noun are similar (for a detailed discussion see Maḫzūmī, *Naḥw* 136-137).

8- The declension of the imperfect is specified with *al-rafᶜ* "the indicative mood" that corresponds to the nominative case of the nouns, *al-naṣb* "the subjunctive mood" that corresponds to the accusative case of the nouns and *al-ğazm* "the jussive mood" that corresponds to *al-ğarr* "the genitive case" of the nouns.

The question of the declinability of the imperfect has been discussed by the Kufans and Basrans (cf. Zağğāğī, *Iḍāḥ* 80-82, Ibn al-Anbārī, *Inṣāf* Q. 73, 224-225, ᶜUkbarī, *Masāᵓil* 83-85, Ibn Yaᶜīš, VII, 12-14). The opinion of the Kufans concerning its declinability differs slightly from the Basrans. They agreed with the Basrans that the imperfect should be declinable, but believed that its declinability is original. By introducing this idea, they opposed the rule that the declinability is principal for the nouns, and assumed that it can as well apply to the verbs as in the case of the imperfect. Their main argument is that the imperfect could refer to different tenses, as the future or a continuous time in the sentences. As well as the use of the three moods, the indicative, subjunctive or jussive, imposes on it different significations. This flexibility similar to the noun's flexibility is according to them the reason of its original declinability.

1.5.1. The forms of the imperfect

The forms of the imperfect *yafᶜalu* are the following:

	sing.	dual	pl.
1st	*ᵓa-fᶜalu*		*na-fᶜalu*
2nd masc.	*ta-fᶜalu*	*ta-fᶜal(a)-āni*	*ta-fᶜal(u)-ūna*
2nd fem.	*ta-fᶜal(i)-īna*	*ta-fᶜal(a)-āni*	*ta-fᶜal-na*
3rd masc.	*ya-fᶜalu*	*ya-fᶜal(a)-āni*	*ya-fᶜal(u)-ūna*
3rd fem.	*ta-fᶜalu*	*ta-fᶜal(a)-āni*	*ya-fᶜal-na*

1.5.1.1. Some remarks concerning its forms:

The imperfect takes prefixes and in some cases infixes and suffixes which refer to the agent. The four prefixes of the imperfect are: the vowelled hamza, *t, y* and *n.* These segments can be combined in different mnemonic words (cf. Ibn Mālik, *Lāmīya* 238, Volck/Kellgren, *Ibn Mālik* 10, Wright, II, 56): e.g. *ʾanaytu* or *naʾtī.*

The forms that I discuss at first are those with the imperfect prefixes vowelled by a fatḥa. Among them I take up the forms with infixes and suffixes. Then I shall discuss the forms with the imperfect prefixes vowelled by a ḍamma in the derived forms and with a kasra in the dialectal variant *al-taltala.*

1.5.1.1.1. The forms with the imperfect prefixes vowelled by a fatḥa:

The imperfect prefixes are vowelled by a fatḥa in Form I of the active voice *ʾa-fʿalu, ta-fʿalu, ya-fʿalu* and *na-fʿalu* on account of the lightness of the fatḥa, and also in the forms constituted of five segments or more in order to alleviate (cf. Åkesson, *Ibn Masʿūd* 68: fol. 10b). The forms that are constituted of five segments or more are the derived forms of the triliteral, namely Form V *ya-tafaʿʿalu,* Form VI *ya-tafāʿalu,*

Form VII *ya-nfa*^{c}*ilu,* Form VIII *ya-fta*^{c}*ilu,* Form IX *ya-f*^{c}*allu,* Form X *ya-staf*^{c}*ilu* etc., and the derived forms of the quadriliteral, namely Form II *ya-tafa*^{c}*lalu,* Form III *ya-f*^{c}*anlilu,* Form IV *ya-f*^{c}*alillu and* Form V *ya-f*^{c}*allilu.*

An anomaly that can be mentioned in which the imperfect prefix is vowelled by a ḍamma, and not by a fatḥa, is *yu-harīqu* "to spill" from *ʾahraqa,* that seems to be formed of five segments. It is basically Form IV *yu-rīqu* from *ʾarwaqa,* in which the *h* is anomalously infixed as a reaction to the phonological change that its middle weak radical has been subjected to (cf. Ibn Ǧinnī, *Sirr I,* 201).

1- *ʾa-f*^{c}*alu:*

An agreement can be noted betwen the *ʾa* that is chosen as an imperfect prefix for the 1st person of the sing. *ʾaf*^{c}*alu* "I do" and the *ʾa* prefix of the independent pronoun of the 1st person of the sing. *ʾanā* "I" (cf. Åkesson, *Ibn Mas*^{c}*ūd* 66: fol. 10a).

2- *ta-f*^{c}*alu:*

The form *ta-f*^{c}*alu* is common for both the 2nd person of the masc. sing. and the 3rd person of the fem. sing.

An agreement can be noted betwen the *ta-* that is chosen as an imperfect prefix for the 2nd person of the masc. sing. *ta-f*ᶜ*alu* "you do" and the *-ta* suffix of the independent pronoun of the 2nd person of the masc. sing. *ᵓan-ta.*

Furthermore the *t-* of the 3rd person of the fem. sing. *ta-f*ᶜ*alu* "she does" and the *-t* suffix of the perfect form *fa*ᶜ*ala-t* "she did" is the same (cf. Wright, *Comparative Grammar* 184). However differently from the voweless *-t* suffix of the perfect *fa*ᶜ*ala-t,* the *t-* prefix of the imperfect is given a vowel because by principle it is impossible to begin the word with a vowelless segment (cf. Åkesson, *Ibn Mas*ᶜ*ūd* 68: fol. 11a).

3- *ya-f*ᶜ*al-na:*

The *ya-* prefix is chosen for the 3rd person of the fem. pl. *ya-f*ᶜ*al-na* and not the *ta-* prefix as in its singular form *ta-f*ᶜ*alu,* to avoid the combination of two markers of the fem., i.e. the *-ta* prefix and the *-na* suffix, which is deemed as heavy in the same verb (cf. ibid, 70: fol. 11b).

4- *ta-f*ᶜ*al(i)-īna, taf*ᶜ*al(u)-ūna, yaf*ᶜ*al(u)-ūna, taf*ᶜ*al(a)-āni, yaf*ᶜ*al(a)-āni:*

a- The *-ī* infix in *ta-f*ᶜ*al(i)-īna* and the *-ū* infix in *taf*ᶜ*al(u)-ūna* and *yaf*ᶜ*al(u)-ūna:*

The *-ī* infix in *ta-f*ᶜ*al(i)-īna* "you do /fem. sing." is the agent pronoun of the 2nd person of the fem. sing. according to the majority of the grammarians with the exception of al-Aḫfaš (cf. ibid, 62: fol. 8b). It detains the same position as an agent, alike the *-ū* infix which is the agent pronoun of the 2nd person of the masc. pl. in *ta-f*ᶜ*al(u)-ūna* "you do / masc. pl." and of the 3rd person of the masc. pl. in *ya-f*ᶜ*al(u)-ūna* "they do /masc. pl.". Al-Aḫfaš prefers to consider the *-ī* infix as a marker of feminization and regards the form *ta-f*ᶜ*al(i)-īna* as having a latent pronoun. His theory is based on the fact that both the 2nd person of the masc. and the 3rd person of the fem. sing. of the imperfect *ta-f*ᶜ*alu* are common and lack a prominent pronoun. It is on this basis and for the sake of analogy that al-Aḫfaš insisted in having the sings. of the imperfect as treated uniformly (cf. Howell, I, fasc. II, 519).

The choice of the *-ī* infix in this form that is specific for the fem. is justified by Ibn Masᶜūd (Åkesson, *Ibn Mas*ᶜ*ūd* 62: fol. 8b) who compares it with the *-ī* that replaces the *-hi* that marks the fem. sing. in the demonstratif pronoun *hāḏihi* which becomes *hāḏ(i)ī* in the expression *hāḏī* ᵓ*amatu l-lāhi* "this is

God's maid-servant" (for this substitution see Rāzī, in Ḫalīl b. Aḥmad ..., *Ḥurūf* 154, Sībawaihi, II, 341, Ibn Ǧinnī, *Sirr II,* 556, Zamaḫšarī, 176). This implies a closeness between the *hi* and the *ī* in marking the feminization and makes the *-ī* fit to be a marker of the fem. Furthermore, the *-ī* infix is necessary so that the sing. form *ta-fᶜal(i)-īna* would be distinguished from the pl. form of the fem. *ta-fᶜal-na* "you do /fem. pl." (cf. Åkesson, *Ibn Masᶜūd* 62: fol. 8b).

b- The *-na* suffix in *ta-fᶜal(i)-īna, tafᶜal(u)-ūna, yafᶜal(u)-ūna,* and the *-ni* suffix in *tafᶜal(a)-āni, yafᶜal(a)-āni:*

The *-na* suffix in the endings *-īna* of the imperfect's form of the 2nd person of the fem. sing. *ta-fᶜal(i)-īna* and *-ūna* of the 2nd and 3rd person of the masc. pl. *ta-fᶜal(u)-ūna* and *ya-fᶜal(u)-ūna* respectively, is the marker of the indicative. It is elided in the jussive and subjunctive mood. It is different from the *-na* suffix attached to the 2nd and 3rd person of the fem. pl. *ta-fᶜal-na* "you do /fem. pl." and *ya-fᶜal-na* "they do /fem. pl.", which in these forms is the marker of the fem. pl. alike the *-na* suffix in the 3rd person of the fem. pl. of the perfect *faᶜal-na* "they did /fem. pl.".

The *-ni* suffix in the ending *-āni* in the dual forms of the 2nd and 3rd persons *ta-f*^{c}*al(a)-āni* and *ya-f*^{c}*al(a)-āni* respectively is also the marker of the indicative.

c- The *-ā* infix in the ending *-āni* in *ta-f*^{c}*al(a)-āni* and *ya-f*^{c}*al(a)-āni:*

The *-ā* infix of the ending -āni in the dual forms of the 2nd and 3rd persons *ta-f*^{c}*al(a)-āni* and *ya-f*^{c}*al(a)-āni* respectively, is the agent pronoun alike the suffix *-ā* of the dual of the perfect of the same persons, namely *fa*^{c}*al-tum(a)-ā* and *fa*^{c}*al(a)-ā* respectively.

The ending *-āni* in these forms is the same as the ending *-āni* of the dual in the noun, e.g. *ḍārib(a)-āni* "hitting /masc. dual". However, differently from the noun in which this ending marks the case of the nominative, and varies to the ending *-ayni* in the cases of the accusative and genitive, namely *ḍāriba-yni,* the ending *-āni* in the imperfect does not vary on the basis that the *-ā* infix is the agent pronoun (cf. ibid, 64: fol. 9a), and the pronoun is invariable.

5- *na-f^{c}alu:*

The *na-* prefix is chosen in the imperfect's form *na-f^{c}alu* of the 1st person of the pl. on the analogy of its choice as the first segment in the ending *-nā* of the perfect *fa^{c}al-nā* "we did" (cf. ibid, 66: fol. 10a).

1.5.1.1.2. The vowelling of the imperfect prefixes with a damma:

The imperfect prefixes are vowelled by a ḍamma in the forms that are formed of four segments (cf. ibid, 68: fol. 10b), which are:

1- Form II of the triliteral: *fa^{cc}ala* > *yu-fa^{cc}ilu* [with double 2nd radical].

2- Form III of the triliteral: *fā^{c}ala* > *yu-fā^{c}ilu.*

3- Form IV of the triliteral: *ʾaf^{c}ala* > *yu-f^{c}ilu.*

Furthermore they are vowelled by a ḍamma in the passive voice Form I *yu-f^{c}alu,* Form II *yu-fa^{cc}alu,* Form III *yu-fā^{c}alu* etc.

<u>1.5.1.1.3. The vowelling of the imperfect prefixes with a kasra:</u>

The imperfect prefixes are vowelled by a kasra in the dialectal variant known as the *taltala* (cf. Rabin, 61). The following forms can be mentioned that take a kasra in this dialect:

1- Form I *faᶜila ya-fᶜalu,* namely *yi-fᶜalu* "you do" in which the imperfect prefix is given a kasra to conform it with the kasra of the 2nd radical of its perfect *faᶜila.* An example is *ᶜalima yaᶜlamu* "to know" in which the kasra of the imperfect prefixes gives notice of the kasra of the 2nd radical of the perfect *ᶜalima,* namely *ᵓi-ᶜlamu* "I know", *ti-ᶜlamu* "/2 masc. and 3 fem. sing.", *yi-ᶜlamu* "/3 masc. sing" and ni-ᶜlamu "/1st pl." (cf. Åkesson, *Ibn Masᶜūd* 68: fol. 10b).

2- Form V *tafaᶜᶜala ya-tafaᶜᶜalu*, namely in the 2nd person of the masc. sing. or the 3rd person of the fem. sing. *ti-tafaᶜᶜalu*, e.g. *ti-takallamu* "you talk or she talks" (cf. Volck/Kellgren, *Ibn Mālik* 11).

3- Form VII *ᵓinfaᶜala ya-nfaᶜilu* namely in the 2nd person of the masc. sing. or the 3rd person of the fem. sing. *ti-nfaᶜilu,* e.g. *ti-nṭaliqu* "you dash along or she dashes along" (cf. ibid).

4- Form X *ᵓistafᶜala ya-stafᶜilu,* namely *yi-stafᶜilu,* e.g. *ᵓistanṣara ya-stanṣiru* "to ask for assistance", namely *yi-*

stanṣiru "he asks for assistance", *ti-stanṣiru* "/2masc. sing." and "3 fem. sing.", *ʾi-stanṣiru* "/1 sing." and *ni-stanṣiru* "1 pl." (cf. Åkesson, *Ibn Masᶜūd* 68: fol. 10b).

5- Form II of the quadriliteral *tafaᶜlala ya-tafaᶜlalu,* namely in the 2nd person of the masc. sing. or the 3rd person of the fem. sing. *ti-tafaᶜlalu,* e.g. *ti-tadaḥrağu* "you roll along, or she rolls along" (cf. Volck/Kellgren, *Ibn Mālik* 11).

1.6. The imperative

The imperative, *al-ʾamr* (for a study see Zamaḫšarī, 114-115, Åkesson, *Ibn Masʿūd* 72 sqq.: 11b sqq., Howell, II-III, 88-96, Wright, II, 61-62, Blachère, 46-47) is a mood through which the action is ordered from the subject. Its pattern is *ʾifʿal,* e.g. *ʾiḍrib* "hit!".

1.6a. The undeclinability of the imperative:

The imperative is undeclinable according to the Basrans (for their opinion see Ibn Ǧinnī, *Ḫaṣāʾiṣ III,* 83, Suyūṭī, *Ašbāh II,* 353-354). Its last radical is given the sukūn, which is a marker that is not given to the noun, - except in the pause which is a special case -, because its does not offer any similarity nor in meaning and nor in form, with the noun (cf. Ibn Yaʿīš, VII, 4).

However according to the Kufans the imperative is underlyingly declinable rather than undeclinable, as they only recognize the imperative as being a part of the declinable imperfect, as it is originally by them an imperfect preceded by the *li-* of command (for discussions see Ḥadīṯī, *Nuḥāt* 84). So the loss of the last vowel is a process which is similar to the case of the declinable imperfect that is put in the jussive mood when it follows the *li-* of the imperative, e.g. *li-yafʿal* "let him do" (cf.

for the Kufans' opinion Farrāʾ, *Maᶜānī I,* 491, Ṯaᶜlab, *Maǧālis II,* 456; for the debate see Ibn al-Anbārī, *Inṣāf* Q. 72, 214-224, *Asrār* 125-126, Zamaḫšarī, 114-115, ᶜUkbarī, *Masāʾil* 114-119, Ibn Yaᶜīš, VII, 61-62).

1.6.1. The forms of the imperative

The imperative is formed by eliding the *li-* of command together with the imperfect prefix of the 2nd persons. Then the connective hamza is prefixed instead of the imperfect prefix. Thus *li-tafᶜal* becomes *ʾifᶜal,* etc.

The forms of the imperative *ʾifᶜal* are the following:

	sing.	dual	pl.
2nd masc.	*ʾifᶜal*	*ʾifᶜal(a)-ā*	*ʾifᶜal(u)-ū*
2nd fem.	*ʾifᶜal(i)-ī*	*ʾifᶜal(a)-ā*	*ʾifᶜal-na*

1.6.1.1. The li- of command:

The *li–* of command that is followed by a verb in the jussive mood, e.g. *li-yafᶜal* "let him do!" resembles the preposition *li-* (cf. Åkesson, *Ibn Masᶜūd* 72: fol 12a) that is followed by a noun in the genitive, e.g. *li-Zaydin* "for Zayd" as both lāms are given a kasra. The verb in the jussive mood corresponds to the noun put in the genitive case (cf. Sībawaihi, I, 4). It can be remarked furthermore that nouns cannot be put in the jussive mood in the same manner as verbs cannot be put in the genitive case (cf. Carter, *Linguistics* [Širbīnī, *Āǧurrūmīya]* 40, 42).

The *li-* is made vowelless by the conjunction *wa-* e.g. *wa-l-yaḍrib* "and let him hit!" said instead of *wa-li-yaḍrib* and *fa-* e.g. *fa-l-yaḍrib* "then let him hit" said instead of *fa-li-yaḍrib* (cf. Åkesson, *Elision* 21).

1.6.1.2. The vowelling of the prefixed connective hamza of the imperative:

According to the Basrans the connective hamza is by principle given the kasra whereas according to the Kufans the connective hamza should follow in its vowel the vowel of the 2nd radical of the verb (for this debate see Ibn al-Anbārī, *Inṣāf* Q. 107, 309-312). According to others the connective prefixed hamza should by principle be vowelless because it is a prefix and it is prior to consider a prefix as being vowelless than vowelled (cf. ibid, Q. 107, 309-312).

The connective hamza is not given the kasra but a ḍamma when the 2nd radical is vowelled by a ḍamma, e.g. *ᵓuktub* "write!" and not *ᵓiktub,* for the sake of analogy (cf. Åkesson, *Ibn Masᶜūd* 74: fol. 12a).

1.7. The Energetic of the imperfect and imperative

The Energetic is formed by giving the termination *-anna* or *-an* (cf. Zamaḫšarī, 155, Ibn Yaᶜīš, IX 37-45, Ibn ᶜAqīl, II, 308-319, Åkesson, *Ibn Masᶜūd* 76-78: fol. 13a-13b, Wright, II, 61, Vernier, I, 32) to the imperfect jussive or to the imperative. The termination *-anna* refers to the Energetic I forms of the imperfect and imperative and the termination *-an* to the Energetic II forms of the imperfect and of the imperative. The Energetic is used to intensify the order in some cases (cf. Sībawaihi, II, 152 sqq., Åkesson, *Ibn Masᶜūd* 76-78: fol. 13b, Vernier, I 40-42), among which the following.

1- The imperative, e.g *ᵓiḍribanna* "hit! /2 masc. sing. (imperative En. I.)" and *ᵓiḍriban* (imperative En. II).

2- The prohibition, e.g. *lā taḍribanna* "do not hit!" (imperfect En. I.) and *lā taḍriban* "do not hit!" (imperfect En. II).

3- The interrogation, e.g. *hal taḍribanna* "will you hit?" (imperfect En. I.) and *hal taḍriban* (imperfect En. II).

4- The optative, e.g. *laytaka taḍribanna* "I wish you would hit" (imperfect En. I.) and *laytaka taḍriban* (imperfect En. II).

5- The request, e.g. *ᵓalā taḍribanna* "are you not going to hit?" (imperfect En. I.) and *ᵓalā taḍriban* (imperfect En. II).

6- The oath, e.g. *wa-l-lāhi lā taḍribanna* "by God, do not hit!" (imperfect En. I.) and *wa-l-lāhi lā taḍriban* (imperfect En. II).

1.7.1. The forms of the Energetic

The forms of the Energetic are divided between the Energetic I of the imperfect of the jussive *yaf^{c}ala-nna,* the Energetic II of the imperfect of the jussive *yaf^{c}ala-n*, the Energetic I of the imperative *ʾi-f^{c}ala-nna* and the Energetic II of the imperative *ʾi-f^{c}ala-n.*

1- The Energetic I of the imperfect of the jussive *yaf^{c}ala-nna:*

The forms of the Energetic I of the imperfect of the jussive *yaf^{c}ala-nna* are the following:

	sing.	dual	pl.
1st	*ʾa-f^{c}ala-nna*		*na-f^{c}ala-nna*
2nd masc.	*ta-f^{c}ala-nna*	*ta-f^{c}al(a)-ānni*	*ta-f^{c}alu-nna*
2nd fem.	*ta-f^{c}ali-nna*	*ta-f^{c}al(a)-ānni*	*ta-f^{c}al-n(a)-ānni*
3rd masc.	*ya-f^{c}ala-nna*	*ya-f^{c}al(a)-ānni*	*ya-f^{c}alu-nna*
3rd fem.	*ta-f^{c}ala-nna*	*ta-f^{c}al(a)-ānni*	*ya-f^{c}al-n(a)-ānni*

2- The Energetic II of the imperfect of the jussive *yafᶜala-n:*

The forms of the Energetic II of the imperfect of the jussive *yafᶜala-n* are the following:

	sing.	dual	pl.
1st	*ʾa-fᶜala-n*		*na-fᶜala-n*
2nd masc.	*ta-fᶜala-n*		*ta-fᶜalu-n*
2nd fem.	*ta-fᶜali-n*		
3rd masc.	*ya-fᶜala-n*		*ya-fᶜalu-n*
3rd fem.	*ta-fᶜala-n*		

3- The Energetic I of the imperative *ʾi-fᶜala-nna:*

The forms of the Energetic I of the imperative *ʾi-fᶜala-nna* are the following:

	sing.	dual	pl.
2nd masc	*ʾi-fᶜala-nna*	*ʾi-fᶜal(a)-ānni*	*ʾi-fᶜalu-nna*
2nd fem..	*ʾi-fᶜali-nna*	*ʾi-fᶜal(a)-ānni*	*ʾi-fᶜal-n(a)-ānni*

4- The Energetic II of the imperative *ʾi-fʿala-n:*

The forms of the Energetic II of the imperative *ʾi-fʿala-n* are the following:

	sing.	dual	pl.
2nd masc	*ʾi-fʿala-n*		*ʾi-fʿalu-n*
2nd fem..	*ʾi-fʿali-n*		

1.7.1.2. Some remarks concerning some of the Energetic's forms:

The forms that I take up at first are those to which the doubled or single *n* is suffixed to without the insertion of any infix or with the elision of one. In these cases, the Energetic's 3rd radical can be vowelled by a fatḥa as in the 3rd persons of the masc sing. *ya-fʿala-nna* and *ya-fʿala-n,* a ḍamma as in the 3rd persons of the masc pl. *ya-fʿalu-nna* and *ya-fʿalu-n* or a kasra as in the 2nd persons of the fem. sing. *ta-fʿali-nna, ta-fʿali-n, ʾi-fʿali-nna* and *ʾi-fʿali-n.* I then discuss the forms with an infix preceding the doubled or single *n* together with a kasra vowelling the nūns instead of the fatḥa, as the infix *ā* of the dual of the 2nd persons of the dual *ta-fʿal(a)-ānni* and *ʾi-fʿal(a)-ānni,* and the inserted *ā* between the *-na* marker of the 3rd person of the fem. pl. and the doubled *n* in the 3rd person of the fem. pl. *ya-f^cal-n(a)-ānni* and *ʾi-f^cal-n(a)-ānni.*

1- The 3rd persons of the masc sing.: ya-fᶜala-nna and ya-fᶜala-n:

The 3rd radical, which is vowelless in the imperfect jussive *li-yafᶜal* "let him do!" and in the imperative *ʾifᶜal* "do!", is given a fatḥa when the doubled *n* of the Energetic I is suffixed to it. Hence *ya-fᶜala-nna* is said and not *ya-fᶜal-nna* to hinder the cluster of two vowelless segments (cf. Åkesson, *Ibn Masᶜūd* 76: fol. 13a). The form referring to the Energetic II with the suffixation of the single *n,* i.e. *ya-fᶜala-n*, follows it in its form.

2- The 3rd persons of the masc pl.: ya-fᶜalu-nna and ya-fᶜalu-n:

The *-ū* suffix of the masc. pl. which is added in the imperfect jussive *li-yafᶜal(u)-ū* "let them do!" and in the imperative *ʾifᶜal(u)-ū* "do!", is elided when the doubled *n* of the Energetic I is suffixed to the form. Hence *ya-fᶜalu-nna* is said and not *ya-fᶜalu-(ū)nna* to alleviate. The form referring to the Energetic II with the suffixation of the single *n,* i.e. *ya-fᶜalu-n* follows it in its form.

3- The 2nd persons of the fem. sing.: ta-f^c^ali-nna, ta-f^c^ali-n, ^ɔ^i-f^c^ali-nna and *^ɔ^i-f^c^ali-n:*

The *-ī* suffix of the fem. sing. which is added in the imperfect jussive *li-taf^c^al(i)-ī* "let her do!" and in the imperative *^ɔ^if^c^al(i)-ī* "do!", is elided when the doubled *n* of the Energetic I is suffixed to the form. Hence *ta-f^c^ali-nna* is said and not *ta-f^c^ali-(ī)nna* (cf. ibid), to alleviate. The forms referring to the Energetic II with the suffixation of the single *n,* i.e. *ta-f^c^ali-n* and to the imperative Energetic I *^ɔ^i-f^c^ali-nna* and Energetic II *^ɔ^i-f^c^ali-n* follow it in their forms.

4- The 2nd persons of the dual: ta-f^c^al(a)-ānni and ^ɔ^i-f^c^al(a)-ānni:

The *-ā* suffix of the dual which is added in the imperfect jussive *li-taf^c^al(a)-ā* "let her do!" and in the imperative *^ɔ^if^c^al(a)-ā* "do!", is not elided when the doubled *n* of the Energetic I is suffixed to the form. The reason of that is to avoid ambiguity with the sing. form (cf. ibid 76: fol. 13a) *ya-f^c^ala-nna*. Another reason why the *-ā* is not elided is according to Ibn ^c^Aqīl, II, 314, its lightness. Furthermore the double *n* is given a kasra and not a fatḥa because of its resemblance to the *n* given a kasra after the *ā* of the dual (cf. Åkesson, *Ibn Mas^c^ūd* 76: fols. 13a-13b) of the termination *-āni* added to the imperfect *ya-fᶜal(a)-āni.* Hence *ta-fᶜal(a)-ānni* is said and not *ta-fᶜala-nna.* The form referring to the imperative Energetic I with the suffixation of the single *n,* i.e. *ᵓi-fᶜal(a)-ānni* follows it in its form.

The suffixation of the single *-n* is not carried out in the imperfect and in the imperative Energetic II to hinder the combination of the vowelless *ā* suffix of the dual and the vowelles single *-n* (cf. Åkesson, *Ibn Masᶜūd* 76: fol. 13b). Hence the forms *ta-fᶜal(a)-ān* and *ᵓi-fᶜal(a)-ān* are not existent by the majority of the grammarians, except by Yūnus and some of his Kufan followers (cf. Sībawaihi, II, 160, Ibn al-Sarrāǧ, *Uṣūl II,* 203, Ibn al-Anbārī, *Inṣāf* Q. 94, 271-277, Zamaḫšarī, 155, Ibn Yaᶜīš, IX, 37-38, Ibn ᶜAqīl, II, 315-316, Åkesson, *Ibn Masᶜūd* 76: fol. 13b).

5- The 3rd person of the fem. pl.: ya-fᶜal-n(a)-ānni and ᵓi-fᶜal-n(a)-ānni:

The *-ā* infix is inserted between the *-na* marker of the 3rd person of the fem. pl. and the doubled *n* to avoid the combination of the nūns (cf. Ibn ᶜAqīl, II, 316, Åkesson, *Ibn Masᶜūd* 76: fol. 13b). Hence *ya-fᶜal-n(a)-ānni* is said and not *ya-fᶜal-n(a)-nni.* The form referring to the imperative Energetic I with the suffixation of the single *n,* i.e. *ᵓi-fᶜal-n(a)-ānni* follows it in its form.

The suffixation of the single *-n* is not carried out in this person in the imperfect and in the imperative Energetic II to hinder the combination of the inserted vowelless *ā* and the vowelles single *-n*. Hence *ya-f^c^al-n(a)-ān* and *^ɔ^i-f^c^al-n(a)-ān* are not existent.

1.8. The passive voice

The passive voice, *al-mağhūl* (cf. Zamaḫšarī, 116-117, Ibn Yaᶜīš, VII, 69-73, Åkesson, *Ibn Masᶜūd* 78: fols 13b-14a, Howell, II-III 120-132) is the form of the verb that expresses the submission of the object to a certain action. The purpose of using it is either to express the baseness of the subject, its sublimity, celebrity, anonymity, the dread from it or the fearing for it.

Its pattern of the perfect is *fuᶜila* and of the imperfect *yufᶜalu.*

1.8.1. The patterns of the derived forms of the triliteral and Form I of the quadriliteral and its derived forms

1- Form II *fuᶜᶜila yufaᶜᶜalu,* e.g. "to be cut".

2- Form III *fūᶜila yufāᶜalu,* e.g. *qūtila yuqātalu* "to be fought".

3- Form IV *ᵓufᶜila yufᶜalu,* e.g. *ᵓukrima yukramu* "to be honoured".

4- Form V *tufuᶜᶜila yutafᶜᶜalu,* e.g. *tuquttila yutaqattalu* "to be fought".

5- Form VI *tufūᶜila yutafāᶜalu,* e.g. *tuqūtila yutaqātalu* "to be fought".

6- Form VII *ᵓunfuᶜila yunfaᶜalu,* e.g. *ᵓunqutila yunqatalu* "to be killed".

7- Form VIII *ᵓuftuᶜila yuftaᶜalu,* e.g. *ᵓuḥtuqira yuḥtaqaru* "to be despised".

8- Form X *ᵓustufᶜila yustafᶜalu,* e.g. *ᵓustuḫriğa yustaḫrağu* "to be extracted".

1.8.2. The patterns of Form I of the quadriliteral and its derived forms

1- Form I *fuᶜlila yufaᶜlalu,* e.g. *duḥriğa yudaḥrağu* "to be rolled".

- Form II *tufuᶜlila yutafaᶜlalu,* e.g. *tuduḥriğa yutadaḥrağu,* e.g. "to be rolled along".

- Form III *ᵓufᶜunlila yufᶜanlalu,* e.g. *ᵓuḥrunğima yuḥranğamu* "to be gathered together in a mass".

- Form IV *ᵓufᶜulilla yufᶜalallu,* e.g. *ᵓuqšuᶜirra yuqšaᶜarru* "to be shuddered with horror".

1.9. The active participle

The active participle (for a study see Zamaḫšarī, 99-101, Ibn Ya^{c}īš, VI, 68-80, Åkesson, *Ibn Mas^{c}ūd* 80-84: fols. 14b-16a, Wright, II, 131-132, Howell, I, fasc. IV, 1606-1650) is a verbal adjective that denotes the "being of the subject" (Bohas/Kouloughli, *Linguistic* 76). It is derived from the imperfect (ibid, 75) because of a similarity that exists between them both.

The active participle has many Form I patterns, the most common among them being *fā^{c}ilun.*

After discussing the similarity of the active participle to the imperfect, I shall present Form I patterns of the triliteral together with the derived forms and Form I pattern of the quadriliteral together with the derived forms. I shall then take up the forms that present a similarity to the active participle, namely the assimilated adjective and the form which is derived from it, namely the elative.

1.9a. The similarity of the active participle to the imperfect:

One similarity that has previously been taken up (cf. par. 1.7a.). is that the phonological form of the imperfect *yaḍribu* and of the active participle *ḍ(a)āribun* are commensurable regarding the vowelling or the vowellessness of both these forms' respective consonants.

Another argument is that the active participle becomes similar to the imperfect in its reference to future time when it is used as a subject governing the noun after it in the accusative, as in e.g. *ʾanā qātilun ġulāmaka* "I am going to kill your servant", which has the same meaning as *ʾanā ʾaqtulu ġulāmaka* or *sa-ʾaqtulu ġulāmaka (cf.* Suyūṭī, *Ašbāh III,* 535-536). The active participle in the sense of the future that operates as a verb on the noun by putting it in the accusative, is also termed by the Kufans as *al-fiʿlu l-dāʾim* "the permansive verb", which has been criticized by the Basrans (for discussions including some references to some modern researchers who accept this term and others who refuse it see Rāğiḥī, *Farrāʾ* 115-138).

1.9.1. The patterns of the groundform

The forms that are discussed are: 1- *fāʿilun,* 2- *faʿīlun* and 3- the forms of intensity.

1- *fāʿilun:*

This form is derived from the form *ya-fʿalu* in the imperfect by eliding the imperfect prefix, infixing the *ā* between the 1st and 2nd radical, and vowelling the 2nd radical with a kasra (cf. Åkesson, *Ibn Mas^cūd* 80: fol. 14b). An example is *ḍāribun* "hitting".

<u>2- *fa^cīlun*:</u>

The active participle can occur formed according to the pattern *fa^cīlun,* e.g. *naṣīrun* "helper".

One form is common for the masc. and fem. if the meaning is that of the passive participle *maf^cūlun* (cf. Zamaḫšarī, 83, Ibn Ya^cīš, V, 102, Åkesson, *Ibn Mas^cūd* 82: fol. 15b, de Sacy, I, 351-352, Wright, II, 186, Vernier, I, 368-369, Blachère, 114-116).

Examples are *qatīlun* "murdered" which is common for the masc. and fem. sing., on the basis that it refers to the passive participle masc. sing. *maqtūlu*n or to the fem. sing. *maqtūlatun* and *ǧarīḥun* "wounded" that refers to the passive participle masc. sing. *maǧrūḥun* or to the fem. sing. *maǧrūḥatun.* This rule is broken if the form is taken as a substantive (cf. Åkesson, *Ibn Mas^cūd* 82: fol. 15b, Vernier, I, 370, Wright, II, 186). Examples are *ḏabīḥatun* "a female victim" and *laqīṭatun* "a female foundling" which have a separate masc. form *ḏabīḥun* and *laqīṭun.*

An anomalous example is *qarībun* that is not formed according to the passive participle *mafᶜūlun,* but which in spite of this fact, is common for both the masc. and fem. as it is occurs instead of *qarībatun* in the sur. 7: 54 *ᵓinna raḥmata l-lāhi qarībun mina l-muḥsinīna* "Verily God's mercy is nigh unto them who do well" (cf. Zamaḫšarī, 83, Ibn Yaᶜīš, V, 102, Åkesson, *Ibn Masᶜūd* 82: fol. 15b, Wright, II, 186).

3- The forms of intensity:

The most common form denoting intensification is *faᶜūlun* (cf. Åkesson, *Ibn Masᶜūd* 82: fol. 15b, Wright, II, 136), e.g. *manūᶜun* "one who is offering great resistance".

The masc. and the fem. sing. have one common form if the pattern has the meaning of the active participle *fāᶜilun* (cf. Åkesson, *Ibn Masᶜūd* 82: fol. 15b, Wright, II, 185, Fleisch, *Traité I,* 337). Examples are *ᵓimraᵓatun ṣabūrun" a* patient woman" in whih *ṣabūrun* stands for the active participle *ṣābiratun* and *rağulun ṣabūrun* "a patient man" in which *ṣabūrun* stands for *ṣābirun.*

An anomalous case worth mentioning is *ᶜaduwwatu*n "enemy" (underlyingly *ᶜad(u)ūatun* on the pattern *fa(u)ūlatun)* in the sentence *hiya ᶜaduwwatu l-lāhi* "she is God's enemy" that is on the pattern *fa^{c}ūlun* which, on the basis that it has the meaning of the active participle *fā^{c}ilun,* namely *^{c}ādiyatun,* should not have a separate form for the fem. The reason however of its occurrence in the fem. according to the pattern *fa(u)ūlatun* is that it is compared to its contrary *ṣadīqatun* "friend /fem", which is on the pattern *fa^{c}īlun* (cf. Suyūṭī, *Ašbāh I,* 422, Ibn Manẓūr, IV, 2848, Åkesson, *Ibn Mas^{c}ūd* 82: fol. 15b, Vernier, I, 369, Lane, II, 1980).

The pattern *fa^{c}ūlun* has a separate form for the fem. sing. if it has the meaning of the passive participle participle *maf^{c}ūlun,* e.g. *nāqatun ḥalūbatun* "a she-camel for milking" in which *ḥalūbatun* stands for the passive participle *maḥlūbatun.*

Some other forms of intensity are: *fa^{cc}ālun* (cf. Howell, I, fasc. IV, 1614), e.g. *ṣabbārun* "having an intense degree of patience", *mif^{c}alun* which is common to the instrumental noun and to the pattern that denotes the intensification of the active participle (cf. ibid, 1622), e.g. *miǧḏamun* in the phrase *sayfun miǧḏamun* "a sword which cuts off quickly", *mif^{c}ālun* that refers to one that is accustomed to the act, e.g. *misqāmun* "often diseased", *fi^{cc}īlun,* e.g. *fissīqun* "very sinful", *fu^{cc}ālun,* e.g. *kubbārun* "very large" and *ṭuwwālun* "very tall", *fa^{cc}ālatun,* e.g. *^{c}allāmatun* "very learned" and *nassābatun* "a great genealogist", *fā^{c}ilatun,* e.g. *rāwiyatun* "one who hands down poems or historical facts by oral tradition", *fa^{cc}ūlatun,* e.g. *farrūqatun* "very timid", *fu^{c}alatun,* e.g. *ḍuḥakatun* "prone to laughter", *fu^{c}latun,* e.g. *ḍuḥkatun* "very ridiculous", *mif^{c}ālatun,* e.g. *miǧḏāmatun* "a man who quickly cuts the tie of affection" and *mif^{c}īlun,* e.g. *mi^{c}ṭīrun* "one who uses much perfume".

The patterns *fa^{cc}ālatun, fā^{c}ilatun, fa^{cc}ūlatun, fu^{c}alatun, fu^{c}latun, mif^{c}ālatun, mif^{c}ālun* and *mif^{c}īlun* are common for both the masc. and fem. sing.

An anomalous example is *miskīnatun* "poor /fem. sing." which is formed according to the pattern *mif^{c}īlun* that should not have a separate form for the fem., but which in this case has. The reason is that it is compared to its contrary *faqīratun* "poor" which is formed according to the pattern *fa^{c}īlun* (cf. Sībawaihi, II, 218, Ibn Manẓūr, III, 2056, Åkesson, *Ibn Mas^{c}ūd* 82: fol. 15b, Lane, I, 1395, Vernier, I, 373-374).

1.9.2. The derived forms of the triliteral and the derived forms of the quadriliteral

The active participle of the derived forms of the triliteral verb and Form I and the derived forms of the quadriliteral, is formed according to the form of the imperfect, by replacing the imperfect radical by the mīm vowelled by a ḍamma, namely *mu,* and by having the 2nd radical still vowelled by a kasra (cf. Åkesson,

Ibn Mas^{c}ūd 82-84: fols 15b-16a, Vernier, I, 38, Wright, I, 300-301).

<u>a- The derived forms of the triliteral:</u>

1- Form II *yufa^{cc}ilu* > *mufa^{cc}ilun,* e.g. *yuqaṭṭi^{c}u* > *muqaṭṭi^{c}un* "cutting".

2- Form III *yufā^{c}ilu* > *mufā^{c}ilun,* e.g. *yuqātilu* > *muqātilun* "fighting".

3- Form IV *yuf^{c}ilu* > *muf^{c}ilun,* e.g. *yukrimu* > *mukrimun* "honouring".

4- Form V *yatafa^{cc}alu* > *mutafa^{cc}ilun,* e.g. *yatafaḍḍalu* > *mutafaḍḍilun* "deigning".

5- Form VI *yatafā^{c}alu* > *mutafā^{c}ilun,* e.g. *yataḍārabu* > *mutaḍāribun* "striking".

6- Form VII *yanfa^{c}ilu* > *munfa^{c}ilun,* e.g. *yanṣarifu* > *munṣarifun* "departing".

7- Form VIII *yafta^{c}ilu* > *mufta^{c}ilun,* e.g. *yaḥtaqiru* > *muḥtaqirun* "despising".

8- Form X *yastafᶜilu* > *mustafᶜilun*, e.g. *yastaḫriǧu* > *mustaḫriǧun* "removing".

b- Form I of the quadriliteral and some of its derived forms:

1- Form I *yufaᶜlilu* > *mufaᶜlilun*, e.g. *yudaḥriǧu* > *mudaḥriǧun* "rolling".

2- Form II *yatafaᶜlalu* > *mutafaᶜlilun*, e.g. *yatadaḥraǧu* > *mutadaḥriǧun* "rolling along".

3- Form III *yafᶜanlilu* > *mufᶜanlilun*, e.g. *yaḥranǧimu* > *muḥranǧimun* "gathering together in a mass".

4- Form IV *yafᶜalillu* > *mufᶜalillun*, e.g. *yaqšaᶜirru* > *muqšaᶜirrun* "shuddering with horror".

1.9.2.1. Some anomalous cases:

There exist some anomalous cases of active participles which are not formed according to the patterns of verbs to which they refer to.

An example is Form IV *mushabun* "loquacious in his speech" (cf. Ibn Manẓūr, III, 2131, Åkesson, *Ibn Masᶜūd* 84: fol. 16a, Lane, I, 1450) from Form IV *ʾashaba* "to prolong in the speech", which is formed anomalously according to Form IV of the passive participle muf^{c}alun instead of Form IV of the active participle *muf^{c}ilun.* Another example is *yāfi^{c}un* "a grown-up boy" which is the active participle of the verb of Form IV *^{ɔ}ayfa^{c}a* "to grow up" that is anomalously formed according to the form of the active participle of the verb of Form I *fā^{c}ilun* (cf. Ibn Manẓūr, VI, 4963, Åkesson, *Ibn Mas^{c}ūd* 84: fol. 16a, Vernier, I, 169).

1.10. The assimilated adjective

The assimilated adjective, *al-ṣifa al-mušabbaha* (for a detailed presentation see Zamaḫšarī, 101, Ibn Yaᶜīš, VI, 81 sqq., Åkesson, *Ibn Masᶜūd* 80: fol. 14b-15a, de Sacy, I, 320-321, Wright, II, 133-136, Vernier, I, 211-212) is the adjective that is assimilated to the participles on the basis of its inflection. Its patterns are derived from Form I of the triliteral verb. Some of the principal measures with some examples are the following:

1- *faᶜlun* e.g. *šaksun* "perverse, stubborn".

2- *faᶜalun* e.g. *ḥasanun* "handsome".

3- *faᶜilun* e.g. *fariqun* "fearful" and *ḫašinun* "rough".

4- *fiᶜlun* e.g. *milḥun* "witty".

5- *fuᶜlun* e.g. *ṣulbun* "hard, rigid".

6- *fuᶜulun* e.g. *ǧunubun* "polluted".

7- *fuᶜālun* e.g. *šuǧāᶜun* "courageous".

8- *faᶜlānun* e.g. *ᶜaṭšānun* "thirsty" and *ǧabānun* "coward".

9- *ᵓafᶜalu* e.g. *ᵓaḥwalu* "squinting". This pattern can present forms that are derived either from the conjugation *faᶜila* as the mentioned *ᵓaḥwalu,* or from the dialectal variants *faᶜula* (cf.

Zabīdī, *Tāǧ XXIV*, 124, Åkesson, *Ibn Masʿūd* 80: fol. 14b-15a) or *faʿila*, e.g. *ʾaḥmaqu* "foolish" from *ḥamuqa* / *ḥamiqa*, *ʾaḫraqu* "unskillful" from *ḫaruqa* / *ḫariqa*, *ʾādamu* "brown" from *ʾaduma* / *ʾadima*, *ʾarʿanu* "careless, silly" from *raʿuna* / *raʿina*, *ʾasmaru* "brown" from *samura* / *samira*, *ʾaʿǧafu* "lean, meagre" from *ʿaǧufa* / *ʿaǧifa* and *ʾaʿǧamu* "non-Arab, dumb, speechless" from *ʿaǧuma* / *ʿaǧima* (cf. Astarābāḏī, *Šarḥ al-šāfiya I*, 71).

1.11. The elative form *ᵓafᶜalu*

The elative, *ism al-tafḍīl* (for a study see Åkesson, *Ibn Masᶜūd* 80-82: fol. 15a, Fleisch, *Traité I,* 409-417, Wright, II, 140-143, Blachère, 97-98) is an adjective that denotes the superiority of the active participle. Its form is *ᵓafᶜalu.*

It is derived from Form I of the triliteral, active, *faᶜala* (cf. Åkesson, *Ibn Masᶜūd* 80: fol. 15a, ᶜAbd al-Raḥīm, *Ṣarf* 96).

1.11.1. Some anomalous cases

Some anomalies occur concerning the elative (for discussions concerning them see Sībawaihi, II, 268-269, Zamaḫšarī, 102, Ibn Yaᶜīš, VI, 91-95, Vernier, I, 229-231, Wright, II, 141-143). It is not to be derived from the following forms, namely:

1- from the passive voice's form *fuᶜila.* An anomalous example is however *ᵓazhā,* which is derived from the passive voice *zuhiya,* in the expression *huwa ᵓazhā min dīkin* "he is more self conceited than a cock" (cf. Zamaḫšarī, 102, Howell, I, fasc. IV, 1703, Vernier, I, 230).

2- from the passive participle's form, *mafᶜūlun* because the elative is meant to refer to the agent and not the object (cf. Åkesson, *Ibn Masᶜūd* 80-82: fol. 15a). Some anomalies exist as the adjective *ʾašġalu* derived from the passive participle *mašġūlun* "busy" that is used as an elative in the proverb *ʾašġalu min ḏāti l-naḥiyayni* (cf. Zamaḫšarī, 102, Åkesson, *Ibn Masʿūd* 82: fol. 15a, Freytag, *Proverbia* 687, Lane, I, 1567, Bustānī, *Muḥīṭ* 471).

3- from the verbal adjective's form that denotes colors *ʾafʿalu,* e.g. *ʾaḥmaru* "red", as it is not said *ʾaḥmaru min* "more red than", to avoid ambiguity. The Kufans however allow the elative to be formed of the colors *bayāḍun* "whiteness" and *sawādun* "blackness", i.e. *ʾabyaḍu min* "whiter than" and *ʾaswadu min* "blacker than", whereas the Basrans do not allow it (for the debate see Ibn al-Anbārī, *Inṣāf* Q. 16, 68-70).

4- from the verbal adjective's form that denotes deformities *ʾafʿalu,* e.g. *ʾaʿwaru* "one-eyed", as it is not said *ʾaʿwaru min* "more one eyed than", to avoid ambiguity. Some anomalies occur however as the example of the adjective *ʾaḥmaqu* "stupid" which occurs as an elative in the proverb *ʾaḥmaqu min Habannaqah* "more stupid than Habannaqah"(cf. Zamaḫšarī, 102, Åkesson, *Ibn Masʿūd* 82: fol. 15a, Freytag, *Proverbia II,* 392).

5- from the derived patterns of the triliteral verb because it would be impossible to maintain all of its segments within the pattern *ʾafʿalu* (cf. Åkesson, *Ibn Masʿūd* 80: fol. 15a). Some anomalous cases however exist as the elatives *ʾaʿṭā* "the one who gives more freely" and *ʾawlā* "the one who bestows more liberally", which are formed anomalously from Form IV *ʾaʿṭā* "to give" and *ʾawlā* "to entrust" respectively. They both occur in the example *huwa ʾaʿṭāhum wa-ʾawlāhum* "he is the one among them who gives more freely and bestows more liberally" (cf. ibid 82: fol. 15a). Other examples occur in the sur. 2: 282 *(ḏālikum ʾaqsaṭu ʿinda l-lāhi wa-ʾaqwamu li-l-šahādati)* "It is juster in the sight of God, more suitable as evidence, and more convenient to prevent doubts among yourselves", in which *ʾaqsaṭu* is formed anomalously from Form IV *ʾaqsaṭa* "to act justly" and *ʾaqwamu* from Form IV *ʾaqāma* "to make right".

1.12. The passive participle

The passive participle, *ᵓism al-mafᶜūl* (for a study see Zamaḫšarī, 101, Ibn Yaᶜīš, VI, 80-81, Åkesson, *Ibn Masᶜūd* 86: fols. 16a-16b, Wright, II, 131-132, Howell, I, fasc. IV, 1651-1661), is a verbal noun which is derived from the passive voice of the imperfect *yu-fᶜalu* (cf. Åkesson, *Ibn Masᶜūd* 86: fol. 16a). It denotes the object on whom or on which the act falls upon.

Its pattern in Form I of the triliteral is *mafᶜūlun,* e.g. *maḍrūbun* "he/it is hit /masc. sing.". Its form of the derived patterns of the triliteral and of Form I of the quadriliteral and its derived forms is formed according to the pattern of the imperfect of the passive voice of the implied form, by replacing the imperfect prefix by the *m* vowelled by a ḍamma, i.e. *mu* (for examples see Wright, II, 300-301, Vernier, I, 166-167).

A- The derived forms of the triliteral:

1- Form II *yufaᶜᶜalu* > *mufaᶜᶜalun,* e.g. *yuqaṭṭaᶜu* > *muqaṭṭaᶜun* "cut".

2- Form III *yufāᶜalu* > *mufāᶜalun,* e.g. *yuqātalu* > *muqātalun* "fought".

3- Form IV *yuf^{c}alu* > *muf^{c}alun,* e.g. *yukramu* > *mukramun* "honoured".

4- Form V *yutafa^{cc}alu* > *mutafa^{cc}alun.*

5- Form VI *yutafā^{c}alu* > *mutafā^{c}alun.*

6- Form VII *yunfa^{c}alu* > *munfa^{c}alun.*

7- Form VIII *yufta^{c}alu* > *mufta^{c}alun,* e.g. *yuḥtaqaru* > *muḥtaqarun* "despised".

8- Form X *yustaf^{c}alu* > *mustaf^{c}alun,* e.g. *yustaḫrağu* > *mustaḫrağun* "removed".

<u>B- The groundform and some of the derived forms of the quadriliteral:</u>

1- Form I *yufa^{c}lalu* > *mufa^{c}lalun,* e.g. *yudaḥrağu* > *mudaḥrağun* "rolled".

2- Form II *yutafa^{c}lalu* > *mutafa^{c}lalun,* e.g. *yutadaḥrağu* > *mutadaḥrağun* "rolled along".

3- Form III *yuf^{c}anlalu* > *muf^{c}anlalun.*

4- Form IV *yuf^{c}alallu* > *muf^{c}alallun.*

1.13. The nouns of time and place

The nouns of time and place, *ᵓasmāᵓ al-zamān wa-l-makān* (for a study see Zamaḫšarī, 103-104, Ibn Yaᶜīš, VI, 107-111, Åkesson, *Ibn Masᶜūd* 88: fols. 16b-17a, Wright, II, 124-130, Howell, I, fasc. IV, 1744-1755, Fleisch, *Traité I,* 429-432) are verbal nouns that denote the time or place with respect to the occurrence of the act therin.

Their patterns are divided between *mafᶜalun* and *mafᶜilun.*

An example of the pattern *mafᶜalun* is *maḏhabun* "a place of departure".

The following nouns are formed according to the pattern *mafᶜilun* (for a presentation see Zamaḫšarī, 104, Åkesson, *Ibn Masᶜūd* 88: fol. 17a, Wright, II, 125-126, Vernier, I, 189, Blachère, 95):

1- *mansikun* "a place where a sacrifice is offered during a religious festival". It can be noted that both *mansikun* with the *s* vowelled by a kasra and *mansakun* with it vowelled by a fatḥa have been read of the sur. 22: 67 *(ǧaᶜalnā mansikan)* or *(ǧaᶜalnā mansakan)* "Have We appointed rites and ceremonies" (cf. Muᵓaddib, *Taṣrīf* 124, Ibn Manẓūr, VI, 4412).

2- *maǧzirun* "a place where animals are slaughtered, slaughterhouse".

3- *manbitun* "a place where a plant grows".

4- *maṭliᶜun* "a place of ascent or rising". Both variants *maṭliᶜun* with the kasra given to the ṭ and *maṭlaᶜun* with the fatḥa given to it exist. The variant *maṭliᶜun* is said to be of the dialect of Tamīm and *maṭlaᶜun* is said to be of the dialect of the Ḥiǧāzis (cf. Sībawaihi, II, 264, Volck/Kellgren: *Ibn Mālik* 24, Ibn Manẓūr, VI, 2689).

5- *mašriqun* "a place where the sun rises, the east".

6- *maġribun* "a place where the sun sets, the west".

7- *mafriqun* "a place of division, the crown of the head".

8- *masqiṭun* "a place where anything falls".

9- *maskinun* "a place where one dwells, habitation".

10- *marfiqun* "a place on which one rests, the elbow".

11- *masǧidun* "a place of prostration in prayer, a mosque".

12- *manḫirun* "a place where the breath passes through the nose".

The noun of time is similar to the noun of place, e.g. *maqtalu l-Ḥusayn* "the time or place of killing Ḥusain".

1.14. The noun of instrument

The noun of instrument, *ᵓism al-ᵓāla* (for a study see Zamaḫšarī, 104-105, Ibn Yaᶜīš, VI, 111-112, Åkesson, *Ibn Masᶜūd* 90: fols. 17a-17b, Wright, II, 130-131, Howell, I, fasc. IV, 1756-1759, Fleisch, *Traité I,* 428-429, Blachère, 97), is derived from the imperfect. It denotes the instrument that is used in carrying out the action expressed by the verb. Its common patterns are the following:

1- *mifᶜalun,* e.g. *mibradun* "a file".

2- *mifᶜālun,* e.g. *miftāḥun* "a key" (for a study with examples see Sībawaihi, II, 267, Zamaḫšarī, 104-105, Wright, II, 130).

3- *mifᶜalatun,* e.g. *miknasatun* "a broom".

4- *mufᶜulun,* e.g. *musᶜuṭun* "an instrument for introducing medicine into the nose" *munḫulun* "a sieve" (cf. Sībawaihi, II, 265 Zamaḫšarī, 105, Ibn Mālik, *Lāmīya* 254, Volck/Kellgren, *Ibn Mālik* 26-27, Åkesson, *Ibn Masᶜūd* 90 fols 17a-17b, Wright, II, 131, Vernier, I, 192, Fleisch, *Traité I,* 429) *mudhunun* "a thing [or pot or vase] in which oil, flash or phial was put" and *muduqqun* "a thing with which one bruises, brays or pounds".

Instrumental nouns are also formed on the measure of *mif*^{c}*alun* or *mif*^{c}*alatun.* Hence, the nouns *miğrafatun, miḥassatun* and *miqra*^{c}*atun* combined together formed upon the measure *mif*^{c}*alatun* occur in a verse said by al-Farazdaq in an elegy on a groom, cited by Howell, I, fasc. IV, 1757:

> *"Li-yabki ʾabā l-Ḫansāʾi baġlun wa-baġlatun*
> *wa-miḫlātu sawʾin qad ʾuḍī*^{c}*a ša*^{c}*īruhā*
> *wa-miğrafatun maṭrūḥatun wa-miḥassatun*
> *wa-miqra*^{c}*atun ṣafrāʾu bālin suyūruhā".*
> "Let a he-mule, and a she-mule, and a nose-bag of evil, whose barley has been wasted, and a rejected broom, and a curry comb, and a yellow whip whose thongs are worn out, bewail Abū l-Ḫansāʾ".

Instrumental nouns of the measure *muf*^{c}*ulatun* and *mif*^{c}*ulatun* exist as well, but they are said to be anomalous, e.g. *al-mukḥulatu* "a thing in which there is a preparation of pulverized antimony used for darkening the edges of the eyelids" (cf. Sībawaihi, II, 265) and *al-miḥruḍatu* "a vessel made of wood, or of brass" (cf. Ibn Manẓūr, II, 837, Lane, I, 549.

2. BIBLIOGRAPHY

2.1. Primary sources

ᶜAbd al-Raḥīm, *Ṣarf* = ᶜAbd al-Raḥīm, Saᶜd, *Muqaddamat fī ᶜilm al-ṣarf,* Cairo s.a.

Åkesson, *Ibn Masᶜūd* = Åkesson, J. , *Arabic Morphology and Phonology based on the Marāḥ al-arwāḥ by Aḥmad b. ᶜAlī b. Masᶜūd, Presented with an Introduction, Arabic Edition, English Translation and Commentary,* Leiden 2001.

Astarābāḏī, *Šarḥ al-šāfiya* = Al-Astarābāḏī, Raḍī l-Dīn Muḥammad b. al-Ḥasan, *Šarḥ šāfiyat Ibn al-Ḥāğib,* edited with *Šarḥ šawāhid* written by ᶜAbd al-Qādir al-Baġdādī, 4 vol., Beirut 1395/1975.

Bakkūš, *Taṣrif* = Al-Bakkūš, Ṭ., *al-Taṣrif al-ᶜarabī,* Tunis 1973.

Bustānī, *Muḥīṭ* = Al-Bustānī, B., *Muḥīṭ al-muḥīṭ,* an Arabic-Arabic Dictionary, Libanon 1983.

Carter, *Linguistics [Širbīnī, Āğurrūmīya]* = Carter, M. G., *Arab Linguistics, an introductory classical text with translation and notes,* Amsterdam 1981.

Daqr, *Muᶜğam* = Daqr, ᶜAbd al-Ġanī, *Muᶜğam al-naḥw,* Beirut 1407 A.H. /1986.

Farrā᾽, *Maᶜānī* = Farrā᾽, Abū Zakarīya Yaḥyā b. Ziyād, *Maᶜānī l-qur᾽ān,* 3 vol., Ed. M. Y. Nağatī and M. ᶜA. Nağğār, Cairo 1955-1972.

Freytag, *Proverbia* = Freytag, G. W., *Arabum Proverbia,* T. I. II. III, I. II. Bonnae 1838-43.

Ḥadīṯī, *Nuḥāt* = Al-Ḥadīṯī, Ḫadīğa, *Mawqif al-nuḥāt mina l-iḥtiğāğ bi-l-ḥadīṯ,* Irak 1986.

Ḫalīl b. Aḥmad..., *Ḥurūf* = Ḫalīl b. Aḥmad wa-b. al-Sakīt wa-l-Rāzī, *Ṯalāṯat kutub fī l-ḥurūf,* Ed. R. ᶜAbd al-Tawwāb, Cairo 1982.

Ibn al-Anbārī, *Inṣāf* = Ibn al-Anbārī, Abū l-Barakāt, *Kitāb al-inṣāf fī masāᵓil al-ḫilāf bayna l-naḥwīyīn al-baṣrīyīn wa-l-kūfīyīn: Die grammatischen Schulen von Kufa und Basra,* Ed. G. Weil, Leiden 1913.

Ibn ᶜAqīl = Ibn ᶜAqīl, *Bihāᵓ al-Dīn ᶜAbdallāh, ˇŠarḥ ᶜalā alfīyat Ibn Mālik,* Ed. ᶜA. al-Ḥamīd, 2 vol., undated.

Ibn Fāris, *Ṣāḥibī* = Ibn Fāris, Aḥmad, *al-Ṣāḥibī fī fiqh al-luġa wa-sanan al-ᶜarab fī kalāmihā,* Ed. M. al-Chouémi, (bibliotheca Philologica; I), Beyrouth 1382/1963.

Ibn Ǧinnī, *de Flexione* = Ibn Ǧinnîi, Abū l-Fatḥ ᶜUṯmān, *de Flexione Libellvs,* Ed. G. Hoberg, Lipsiae, 1885.

Ibn Ǧinnī, *Ḫaṣāᵓiṣ* = Ibn Ǧinnī, Abū l-Fatḥ ᶜUṯmān, *al-Ḫaṣāᵓiṣ,* Ed. M. A. al-Naǧǧār, 3 vol., Cairo 1371/1952-1376/1956.

Ibn Ǧinnī, *Munṣif* = Ibn Ǧinnī, Abū l-Fatḥ ᶜUṯmān, *al-Munṣif fī šarḥ taṣrīf al-Māzinī,* Ed. I. Muṣṭafā, ᶜA. Amīn, 3 vol., Cairo 1373/1954-1379/1960.

Ibn Ǧinnī, *Sirr* = Ibn Ǧinnī, Abū l-Fatḥ ᶜUṯmān, *Sirr ṣināᶜat al-iᶜrāb,* Ed. Ḥ. Hindāwī, 2 vol., Damascus 1405/1985.

Ibn Ḫālawaihi, *Iᶜrāb* = Ibn Ḫālawiya, Abū ᶜAbd Allāh al-Ḥusain b. Aḥmad, *Iᶜrāb ṯalāt–īn sūra mina l-Qurᵓān,* Damascus s.a.

Ibn Ḫālawaihi, *Qirāᵓāt* = Ibn Ḫālawaihi, Abū ᶜAbd Allāh al-Ḥusain b. Aḥmad, *Iᶜrāb al-qirāᵓāt al-sabᶜ wa-ᶜilaluhā,* Ed. ᶜAbd al-Raḥmān b. Sulaimān al-ᶜAtīmain, 2 vol., Cairo 1413/1992.

Ibn Mālik, *La Alfiya* = Ibn Mālik, Muḥammad b. ᶜAbd Allāh, *La ᵓAlfiyyah d'Ibnu-Malik* [pp. 1-227], suivie de (->) *La Lāmiyyah* du meme auteur (pp. 228-353) avec traduction et notes en français et un lexique des termes techniques par A. Goguyer, Beyrouth 1888.

Ibn Manẓūr = Ibn Manẓūr, Ǧamāl al-Dīn, *Lisān al-ᶜArab,* 6 vol., Beirut undated.

Ibn al-Sarrāǧ, *ᵓUṣūl* = Ibn al-Sarrāǧ, Abū Bakr, *al-ᵓUṣūl fī l-Naḥw,* Ed. ᶜA. Ḥ. al-Fatlī, Beirut 1408/1988.

Ibn ᶜUṣfūr = Ibn ᶜUṣfūr al-Ašbīlī, Abū l-ᶜAbbās ᶜAlī b. Muᵓmin, *al-Mumtiᶜ fī l-taṣrīf,* Ed. F. al-Dīn Qabāwih, Aleppo 1390/1970.

Ibn Yaᶜīš = Ibn Yaᶜīš, Muwaffaq al-Dīn Abū l-Barāᵓ Yaᶜīš, *Šarḥ al-mufaṣṣal,* 2 vol., Beirut undated.

Ibn Yaᶜīš, *Mulūkī* = Ibn Yaᶜīš, Muwaffaq al-Dīn Abū l-Barāᵓ Yaᶜīš, *Šarḥ al-mulūkī fī l-taṣrīf,* Ed. Faḫr al-Dīn Qabāwa, Aleppo 1393/1973.

Maḫzūmī, *Naḥw* = Al-Maḫzūmī, M., *Fī l-naḥw al-ᶜarabī,* Beirut 1986.

Muᵓaddib, *Taṣrīf* = Al-Muᵓaddib, al-Qāsim b. Muḥammad b. Saᶜīd, *Daqāᵓiq al-taṣrīf,* Ed. A. N. al-Qaisī, Ḥ. Ṣ. al-Ḍāmin and Ḥ. Tūrāl, Iraq 1407/1987.

Rāǧiḥī, *Farrāᵓ* = Al-Rāǧiḥī, Šaraf al-Dīn, *Fī l-muṣṭalaḥ al-ṣarfī ᶜinda l-Farrāᵓfī kitābati "Maᶜānī l-qurᵓān",* Alexandria 1992.

Sībawaihi = Sîbawaihi, Abū Bišr ᶜAmr b. ᶜUṯmān, *Le Livre de Sîbawaihi (Kitāb Sībawaihi), Traité de grammaire arabe,* Ed. H. Derenbourg, 2 vol., Paris 1881-1889. Réimpression: 1970.

Širbīnī, Āğurrūmīya = see Carter, *Linguistics.*

Suyūṭī, *Ašbāh* = Al-Suyūtī, Ǧalāl al-Dīn Abū l-Faḍl ᶜAbd al-Raḥmān, *al-ᵓAšbāh wa-l-naẓāᵓir,* Ed. ᶜAbd Allāh Nabhān, 4 vol., Damascus 1406/1985.

Suyūṭī, *Muzhir* = Al-Suyūtī, Ǧalāl al-Dīn Abū l-Faḍl ᶜAbd al-Raḥmān, *al-Muzhir fī ᶜulūm al-luġa wa-anwāᶜihā,* 2 vol., Cairo undated.

Ṯaᶜlab, *Mağālis* = Ṯaᶜlab, Abū l-ᶜAbbās Aḥmad b. Yaḥyā, *Mağālis,* Ed. ᶜA. al-Salām Hārūn, 1375/1956.

ᶜUkbarī, *Masāᵓil* = Al-ᶜUkbarī, Abd Allāh b. al-Ḥusain, *Masāᵓil ḫilāfīya fī l-naḥw,* Ed. M. Ḫ. al-Ḥalawānī, Aleppo, undated.

Versteegh, *Zağğāğī* = Versteegh, K., *The explanation of linguistic causes. Az-Zağğāğī's theory of grammar. Introduction, translation, commentary,* Amsterdam 1995.

Zabīdī, *Tāğ* = Al-Zabīdī, Muḥammad b. Muḥammad Murtaḍā l-Ḥusainī, *Tāğ al-ᶜarūs min ğawāhir al-qāmūs,* Ed. M. Ḥiğāzī, Kuweit 1369/1969.

Zağğāğī, *Īḍāḥ* = Al-Zağğāğī, Abū Qāsim ᶜAbd al-Raḥmān, *al-Īḍāḥ fī ᶜilal al-naḥw,* Ed. M. al-Mubārak, Cairo 1378/1959.

Zamaḫšarī = Zamaḫs'ario, Abū l-Qāsim Maḥmūd b. ᶜUmar, *al-Mufaṣṣal,* Ed. J. P. Broch, Christianiae 1840.

2.2. Secondary sources

Åkesson, *Elision* = Åkesson, *Anomalous elision and addition of a vowel in Classical Arabic,* in: ZAL 36, Wiesbaden 1999.

Åkesson, *Ibn Masᶜūd* = Åkesson, J., *Arabic Morphology and Phonology based on the Marāḥ al-arwāḥ by Aḥmad b. ᶜAlī b. Masᶜūd, Presented with an Introduction, Arabic Edition, English Translation and Commentary,* Leiden 2001.

Blachère = Blachère, R., et Gaudefroy-Demombynes, M., *Grammaire de l'Arabe classique,* Paris, 1952.

Bohas/Kouloughli, *Linguistic* = Bohas, G., Guillaume, J.-P., Kouloughli, D.E., *The Arabic Linguistic Tradition,* London and New York 1990.

Carter, *Linguistics* [Širbīnī, *Āğurrūmīya]* = Carter, M. G., *Arab Linguistics, an introductory classical text with translation and notes,* Amsterdam 1981.

Fleisch, *Traité I* = Fleisch, H., *Traité de Philologie Arabe, vol. I, Préliminaires, Phonétique Morphologie Nominale,* Beyrouth 1961.

Fleisch, *Traité II* = Fleisch, H., *Traité de Philologie Arabe, vol. II, Pronoms, Morphologie verbale, Particules,* Beyrouth 1979.

Ḥassān, *Uṣūl* = Ḥassān, Tammām, *al-Uṣūl,* Cairo 1982.

Haywood, *Lexicography* = Haywood, J. A., *Arabic lexicography. Its history, and its place in the general history of lexicography*, Leiden 1965.

Howell = Howell, M. S., *Grammar of the Classical Arabic Language,* 4 parts in 7 vol., Allahabad 1880-1911.

Lane = Lane, E.W., *Arabic-English Lexicon,* 8 in 2 vol., London 1863-1893. Reprint: 1984.

Owens, *Foundations* = Owens, J., *The Foundations of Grammar, An Introduction to Medieval Arabic Grammatical Theory,* Amsterdam/ Philadelphia 1988.

Penrice, *Dictionary* = Penrice, J., *A Dictionary and Glossary of the Kor-ân,* London 1873. Reprint: 1971.

Rabin = Rabin, C., *Ancient West-Arabian,* London 1951.

Roman, *Étude* = Roman, A., *Étude de la phonologie et de la morphologie de la koinè arabe,* 2 vol., Publications de l'Université de Provence, Marseille 1983.

De Sacy = De Sacy, S., *Grammaire arabe,* 2 vol., Tunis 1904-1905.

Vernier = Vernier, D., *Grammaire arabe,* 2 vol., Beyrouth 1891.

Versteegh, *Langage* = Versteegh, C. H. M., *The Arabic language,* Edinburgh 1996.

Versteegh, *Zaǧǧāǧī* = Versteegh, K., *The explanation of linguistic causes. Az-Zaǧǧāǧī's theory of grammar. Introduction, translation, commentary,* Amsterdam 1995.

Volck/Kellgren, *Ibn Mālik* = Volck, W., *Ibn Mālik's Lâmîyat al afᶜâl mit Badraddîn's Commentar von Kellgren,* Mémoires de l'académie impériale des sciences de St.-Petersbourg, tome VII, No 6, St. Petersburg 1864.

Vollers, *Volkssprache* = Vollers, K., *Volkssprache und Schriftsprache im alten Arabien,* Strassburg 1906.

Wright = Wright, W., *A Grammar of the Arabic Language,* Cambridge, Third Edition 1985.

Wright, *Comparative Grammar* = Wright, W., *Lectures on the Comparative Grammar of the Semitic Languages*, Cambridge 1890.

3. INDEX OF QUR'ANIC QUOTATIONS

Sur.	v.	page
69:	8	31
56:	2	31
69:	4	31
68:	6	31
31:	11	32
16:	89	32

78:	28	36
53:	31	41
7:	54	78
2:	282	88
22:	67	91

4. INDEX OF VERSES

5. INDEX OF NAMES

ᶜAbd al-Raḥīm 1, 97

ᶜAbd al-Tawwāb 51

Åkesson 1, 2, 8, 9, 20, 35, 36, 40, 47, 50, 51, 53, 54, 55, 57, 58, 59, 63, 64, 65, 66, 67, 70, 71, 72, 73, 75, 76, 80, 81, 82, 84, 86, 88, 89, 90, 91, 92, 93, 94, 95, 96, 97, 98, 100, 102, 105

al-Aḫfaš 46, 51, 66

ᶜĀṣim 9

Astarābāḏī 96

Aus b. Ḥāriṯa b. Laᵓm al-Ṭāᵓī 34

Bakkūš 1

Basrans 3, 4. 5. 6. 7. 61, 72, 74, 87, 98

Bišr b.Abī Ḫāzim 34

Blachère 1, 9, 10, 20, 72, 88, 97, 102, 105

Bohas 42, 86

Bustānī 98

Carter 43, 74

Daqr 37

al-Farazdaq 106

Farrā᾽ 50, 73, 87

Fleisch 9, 20, 24, 25, 26, 29, 89, 97, 102, 105

Freytag 98

Goguyer 56

Ḥadīṯī 72

Ḫalīl 23, 51, 67

Ḥamza 9

Ḥassān 52

Ḥiğāzis 103

Howell 2, 9, 10, 11, 12, 13, 14, 15, 16, 17, 18, 20, 23, 24, 25, 26, 28, 29, 30, 34, 37, 38, 40, 45, 51, 58. 66, 72, 84, 86, 90, 97, 100, 102, 105, 106

Ibn ᶜAmir 9

Ibn al-Anbārī 3, 5, 45, 54, 61, 73, 74, 82, 98

Ibn ᶜAqīl 76, 81, 82

Ibn Fāris 34, 35

Ibn Ğinnī 2, 53, 56, 64, 67, 72

Ibn Ḫālawaihi, 45, 60

Ibn Mālik 23, 24, 25, 26, 28, 29, 30, 36, 38, 56, 63, 70, 71, 103, 105

Ibn Manẓūr 23, 25, 28, 37, 90, 91, 93, 94, 102, 103, 106

Ibn Masᶜūd 1, 2, 8, 9, 20, 35, 36, 40, 47, 50, 51, 53, 54, 55, 57, 58, 59, 63, 64, 65, 66, 67, 70, 71, 72, 73, 75, 76, 80, 81, 82, 84, 86, 88, 89, 90, 91, 92, 93, 94, 95, 96, 97, 98, 100, 102, 105

Ibn al-Sarrāǧ 82

Ibn ᶜUṣfūr 21, 24, 28

Ibn Yaᶜīš 1, 2, 3, 4, 34, 35, 36, 38, 40, 43, 45, 50, 51, 56, 57, 58, 59, 61, 72, 73, 76, 82, 84, 86, 88, 89, 95, 97, 100, 102, 105

Kellgren 22, 23, 24, 25, 26, 28, 29, 36, 38, 63, 70, 71, 103, 105

Kouloughli 42, 86

Kūfans 3, 4, 5, 6, 61, 72, 73, 74, 82, 87, 98

Lane 3, 9, 37, 42, 56, 90, 91, 93, 98, 106

Maḫzūmī 61

al-Māzinī 2

Muʾaddib 1, 45, 54, 102

Owens 42, 59

al-Rāʾī 37

Rabin 40, 70

Rāǧiḥī 87

Rāzī 51, 67

Roman 9, 20

de Sacy 1, 3, 20, 42, 88, 95

Sālim b. Dāra 54

Sībawaihi 5, 8, 9, 10, 11, 13, 14, 16, 17, 18, 30, 36, 57, 67, 74, 76, 91, 97, 103, 105, 106

Širbīnī 43, 74

Suyūṭī 21, 23, 24, 25, 26, 28, 29, 45, 72, 87, 90, 106

Ṯa^{c}lab 73

Tamīm 103

^{c}Ukbarī 3, 6, 42, 61, 73

Vernier 9, 10, 11, 12, 13, 14, 15, 16, 18, 20, 76, 88, 90, 91, 92, 94, 95, 97, 100, 102, 105

Versteegh 43, 48

Volck 22, 23, 24, 25, 26, 28, 29, 36, 38, 63, 70, 71, 103, 105

Vollers 9

Yemenites 40

Yūnus 82

Zabīdī 96

Zaǧǧāǧī 3, 6, 43, 52, 61

Zamaḫšarī 3, 4, 5, 9, 10, 12, 13, 14, 15, 16, 17, 18, 20, 24, 30, 34, 35, 36, 38, 40, 50, 51, 56, 67, 72, 73, 76, 82, 84, 86, 88, 89, 95, 96, 97, 98, 100, 102, 105

www.ingramcontent.com/pod-product-compliance
Lightning Source LLC
Chambersburg PA
CBHW021009090426
42738CB00007B/723
* 9 7 8 9 1 9 7 7 6 4 1 7 9 *